DON'T MISS THIS

IN THE
OLD TESTAMENT

MORE *DON'T MISS THIS* PRODUCTS
FROM EMILY BELLE FREEMAN AND DAVID BUTLER

Don't Miss This Poster Set—Old Testament

Don't Miss This Stickers for Scriptures—Old Testament

Don't Miss This in the Book of Mormon:
Exploring One Verse from Every Chapter

Don't Miss This 2020 Journal:
A Companion to Your Come, Follow Me Book of Mormon Study

Don't Miss This in the Doctrine and Covenants:
Exploring One Verse from Every Chapter

Don't Miss This 2021 Journal:
A Companion to Your Come, Follow Me Doctrine and Covenants Study

Don't Miss This in the Doctrine and Covenants Poster Set

Don't Miss This Stickers for the Doctrine and Covenants

DON'T MISS THIS

IN THE
OLD TESTAMENT

EXPLORING ONE VERSE
FROM (ALMOST) EVERY CHAPTER

EMILY BELLE FREEMAN
and DAVID BUTLER

DESERET
BOOK

Salt Lake City, Utah

Library of Congress Cataloging-in-Publication Data

Names: Freeman, Emily, 1969– author. | Butler, David, author. | Freeman, Emily, 1969– Don't miss this.

Title: Don't miss this in the Old Testament : exploring one verse from (almost) every chapter / Emily Belle Freeman and David Butler.

Other titles: Do not miss this in the Old Testament

Description: Salt Lake City, Utah : Deseret Book, [2021] | Series: Don't miss this | Includes bibliographical references. | Summary: "Latter-day Saint authors Emily Belle Freeman and David Butler continue their Don't Miss This series with the Old Testament, exploring one verse from (almost) every chapter"—Provided by publisher.

Identifiers: LCCN 2021022328 | ISBN 9781629729510 (trade paperback)

Subjects: LCSH: Bible. Old Testament—Commentaries. | Pearl of Great Price. Book of Moses—Commentaries. | The Church of Jesus Christ of Latter-day Saints—Doctrines. | Mormon Church—Doctrines.

Classification: LCC BS1151.52 .F74 2021 | DDC 221.6—dc23

LC record available at https://lccn.loc.gov/2021022328

Printed in the United States of America

LSC Communications, Crawfordsville, IN

10   9   8   7   6   5   4   3   2   1

To Desi and Kingston,
who face battles that seem insurmountable.
He will be there.

—EBF

To Mom—who showed me
a God of promise and deliverance.

—DB

CONTENTS

You'll notice that, although we've listed below the books of the Old Testament in the order in which they appear in scripture, the contents of this book don't always go in that same order. For example, the books of Kings and Chronicles intermingle in much the same way that the four Gospels in the New Testament do—same stories, different tellings. So there will be some jumping around. We've included this Contents guide to help lead you most easily to the books you want.

Another surprise: you'll encounter some content that doesn't come from the Old Testament at all. We've included some entries from the books of Moses and Abraham in the Pearl of Great Price that shed extra light on the book of Genesis. We're grateful for anything that enriches our study of the Old Testament and hope you feel the same way!

OUR HOPE FOR THIS BOOK

We don't know how you will use this book, but maybe it will help if we tell you how we use the book! We leave it out near the kitchen table. We like to read one verse a day with its accompanying devotional at dinner or breakfast time and then talk about the question at the bottom of the page while we eat. It is helping us to make the *Come, Follow Me* program part of our everyday routine. In this particular devotional book you will also find that we refer often to the Hebrew meanings of words. Our most used source for this is *Strong's Concordance*, available in various apps and online. Hebrew is a beautiful and dynamic ancient language, and understanding some of its nuances can open up new understanding and insight about familiar words.

This book is different from other Old Testament books you might have studied. It is not a verse-by-verse guide, nor will we dive deeply into the doctrine. Instead we will read the stories, looking for the inspiration within. As we do this, we believe something remarkable will begin to happen—we will come to understand the individual application these biblical stories can have in our own lives today. The pages of the Old Testament include lessons on building testimony, strengthening family, following the prophet, overcoming great adversity, instilling belief, understanding hope, and finding the courage to sustain us through the great battles of life. We will learn to trust with Gideon, build with Nehemiah, plead with Hezekiah, and stand up for what we know like Micaiah. We will read stories of courageous prophetesses, great women, and mothers in Israel. We will come to realize that the greatest blessings in life cannot come from that which doth cost us nothing. As you come to witness God's deliverance in these pages, we hope it enables you to see His deliverance even more clearly in the pages of your own story.

We absolutely love studying with you, and, more than anything, we pray this book will help make your study of the Old Testament more personal and meaningful this year.

DAVID AND EMILY

INTRODUCTION

People often ask us why the Old Testament is our favorite book of scripture. We would definitely tell you our hearts are won over by the grand heroes and the wild, epic stories of triumph. It is a book filled with the surprising and the extraordinary. But there is more. There will come a moment in your life when you or someone you love will struggle with a challenge so great you will wonder how you will make it through. In that moment, you may long to better understand the Savior's role as the Deliverer. We believe one of the best ways to see Jesus Christ in that role is to turn to the Old Testament. The stories and lessons of the Old Testament have carried us through some of the greatest challenges of our lives. When we need deeper courage, unyielding strength, and increased wisdom to face the situation at hand, we turn to the stories of heroes in the Old Testament. Rather, we turn to the stories of The Hero in the Old Testament. It is within those pages that both of us have come to know Jehovah, the Deliverer—Jesus Christ—in personal and significant ways.

It is common when beginning a study of the Old Testament to immediately feel intimidated by the sheer number of pages, the scriptural language, or even some of the harsh themes. We hope that won't be the case as we begin this study of the Old Testament. Instead, let anticipation begin to fill your heart, because you are about to discover stories you might have missed and heroes you may have never met before, including Jehoshaphat, Mephibosheth, Micaiah, the wise woman of the city, and the daughters of Shallum who ruled the half part of Jerusalem. We cannot wait to introduce you to some of these great women and men we have grown to love and admire. This book isn't big enough to contain all of the chapters in the Old Testament. Instead, we chose our favorites from the years we have taught seminary and institute. You might have read some of these stories or insights before in Emily's book *Written on Our Hearts*. Some of them can be found in the *Come, Follow Me* manual, and some are here because we simply didn't want you to miss the goodness there.

We live in a world that pleads for deliverance. We may not be called upon to cross the Red Sea, find ourselves thrown into a pit and left for dead, or face armies whose strength is far greater than ours. We may not be led into captivity, be compassed on every side by the enemy, or be called upon to testify knowing it might lead to our death. However, there will be days when we face danger, oppression, and injustice. There will be great obstacles in our way and times when we feel surrounded by those who are intent on destroying us. We will face evil, overwhelming health challenges, and perhaps the captivity of sin. In these moments we must remember that, just as the Lord delivered the children of Israel, He has the power to deliver us from any trouble we must overcome in our life. He is, after all, the Great Deliverer. The pages of the Old Testament testify of Him.

In the midst of every challenge or adversity, one thing is certain—the Lord *will* deliver us. The Old Testament will help us understand how.

MOSES 1:6

I have a work for thee.

This morning the rising of the sun seems to celebrate the New Year, shedding light on new beginnings and possibilities that are endless. I begin the day asking the Lord what work He would have me do this year and for the strength to accomplish whatever it is He has in mind. In this moment, I learn from Moses. I follow in his steps. Today my journey is his. I read, "I am the Lord God Almighty, and Endless is my name. . . . And, behold, thou art my son [my daughter] . . . and I have a work for thee" (Moses 1:3–6).

I wonder, *What is that work, Lord? How might I discover it?* Again, I read the words of Moses, "I will not cease to call upon God, I have other things to inquire of him" (Moses 1:18) and I set a resolution: this year I will not cease to call upon God, with the hope that I will be led to discover the work He has in mind for me. *His work.*

But what if it is a challenge that seems bigger than I am? What if I am not equal to the task? His answer brings comfort and instills confidence, "Blessed art thou, . . . for I, the Almighty, have chosen thee, and thou shalt be made stronger" (Moses 1:25).

If the Lord had a work for Moses, then surely He must have a work for each one of us. And if the Lord *knew* Moses and called him Son, then the Lord must *know* you and me. He has promised, "They are mine and I know them" (Moses 1:35). My heart knows the truth of those words. The Lord knows each of us individually. We are His. So today, maybe we could inquire of Him and then open our heart to experience His endless possibilities. Like Moses, we could try to discover the work He has in mind for us. And perhaps, we will be made stronger. —EBF

Reflect and Respond
What is the work God has in mind for you?

Your favorite scripture in **Moses 1**

GENESIS 1:31

And God saw every thing that he had made,
and, behold, **it was very good**.

Have you noticed that every time God created something, He stood back and saw that it was good? It's found in the second chapter of Moses: "And I, God, saw that all things which I had created were good" (Moses 2:21). It is there in Abraham: "He stood among those that were spirits, and he saw that they were good" (Abraham 3:23). And again in Genesis: "And God saw every thing that he had made, and, behold, it was very good" (Genesis 1:31).

What is it about this doctrine that is so important it needed to be repeated three times in a row? One lesson that stands out to me is this: God created *you*. Which means *He knows that you are good*. And not just good, but *very good*.

He believes that about you even on your worst days. So when things don't seem to be going exactly right, you might want to turn to Moses, or Abraham, or Genesis and be reminded, "*God saw every thing that he had made, and, behold, it was very good*."

Perhaps you could also gain strength from another lesson that is repeated in all three chapters: "And I, God, created man in mine own image. . . . And I, God, *blessed them*" (Moses 2:27, 28; emphasis added). "So the Gods went down to organize man in their own image. . . . And the Gods said: *We will bless them*" (Abraham 4:27, 28; emphasis added). And again, "So God created man in his own image. . . . *And God blessed them*" (Genesis 1:27, 28; emphasis added).

The profound thought of God creating us, knowing the good in each of us, and then blessing us gives me courage, and strength, and hope. Perhaps today you are in need of this simple reminder given from the Lord Himself: You are good. You are blessed. Hold on to that today. —EBF

Reflect and Respond
If God were to tell you His favorite quality about you, what do you think it would be?

Your favorite scripture in **Genesis 1**

MOSES 3:18

**It was not good that the man should be alone;
wherefore, I will make an help meet for him.**

After each day of creation, God pronounced that what was done was good. The seas were good, the animals were good, and the flowers were good too. The beaches, the mountains, the sun, the stars—all good. But there was one thing during the days of creation that was not good. It was not good that Adam, man, should be alone. The responsibilities of multiplying, replenishing, ruling, and reigning over the paradise place were to be shared. They were meant to be done together. So a help meet was created for Adam. The English translation of that title given to Eve does not sound very flattering to someone reading it today. "Help meet" just doesn't have much of an elegance to it. But it is actually a beautiful title—fitting for someone like Eve. The original Hebrew phrase, *ezer kenegdo,* is a phrase that could be translated, "a complementary opposite."[1]

Adam and Eve would certainly be different, and almost opposite in many ways, but their differences would be complementary. As an illustration, the right hand can be seen as the *ezer kenegdo* of the left hand. They are opposite of each other, but working together, they are stronger. The left wing of a plane, likewise, is the *ezer kenegdo* of the right. Like the hands, they are different in form, but equal in purpose and power, and better together. In fact, it would not be good for a left wing to be alone.

When Eve was created as a help meet for Adam (and Adam a help meet for Eve), the scriptures say she was symbolically taken from his rib. Perhaps that is a way of teaching us that man and woman were created and called to do a great work side by side. —DB

Reflect and Respond

How have you seen men and women work together as complementary opposites—different in form, but stronger together?

Your favorite scripture in
Moses 3

MOSES 4:15

**And I, the Lord God, called unto Adam,
and said unto him: Where goest thou?**

There were trees of every kind in the Garden of Eden that God told Adam and Eve to eat of freely. There was one, however, that was forbidden—the tree of knowledge of good and evil. If they ate from that one, they would die. According to the story, the serpent came and beguiled Adam and Eve and tempted them to disobey the commandment. After eating the forbidden fruit, Adam and Eve discovered they were naked and were ashamed, so they covered themselves with fig leaves. When they heard the voice of the Father coming near, the two of them hid.

Even though the Lord knew where they were, He still came into the garden and asked an important question of the hiding couple: "Adam . . . where art thou?" (Genesis 3:9). In the Moses account, it is translated a little differently: "Adam . . . where goest thou?" (Moses 4:15).

Our stories today can be so similar. We disobey, try to cover up our problems, run, hide, and blame. It seems like God would still ask us the same question He did to Adam and Eve: "Where art thou?" Or perhaps, in other words: "Where are you spiritually? Are you where you want to be?" And, "Where goest thou?" Or: "Which direction are you facing? And why are you running and hiding from the only One who can actually solve this problem? What did the serpent tell you about me that would make you think I was the kind of Father you would want to run from? Let me show you who I really am." —DB

Reflect and Respond

What do you know about God that would make you want to run toward Him in times of trouble instead of hiding from Him?

Your favorite scripture in **Moses 4**

GENESIS 4:9

Am I my brother's keeper?

Whenever I come across a question in scripture, I like to take a minute to stop reading and ask the question to myself. It's a great way to get a close-up perspective of your heart. In the book of Genesis, God's first recorded question to mankind was, "Where goest thou?" (Moses 4:15). A little later in the story, we get mankind's first recorded question to God.

After Adam and Eve left the Garden of Eden, Satan continued his attempts to overthrow God's plan. He tempted Cain, one of Adam and Eve's sons, with power, jealousy, and anger. He convinced Cain that happiness could be found in ruling over others. Cain listened to the devil's cunning lies, and soon he rose up against his own brother, Abel, and killed him. When the Lord came to Cain after his horrible crime and asked him where his brother was, Cain responded with the question, "Am I my brother's keeper?" (Genesis 4:9). Every time I read that I shiver with sadness. I can almost hear his coarse and loveless tone of voice.

There is no recorded answer to Cain's question, but if someone asked me that question, my answer would be a resounding and enthusiastic, "YES!" It would not just be Adam and Eve who would enter mortality. We all came here to experience it, and we experience it together: both with God and with other people. Perhaps Cain's question is one we should all consider and ask ourselves. Are we our brother's keeper? As we walk through the thorns and thistles of the world, what is our relationship to those with whom we journey? —DB

Reflect and Respond

How would you respond to Cain's question? Are we our brother's keeper?

Your favorite scripture in **Genesis 4**

MOSES 5:11

Were it not for our transgression we never should have . . . known good and evil.

It must have been painful for Adam and Eve to leave their paradise place and enter the dreariness of mortality. The fallen earth would have thorns and thistles, sweat and sorrow, dread and death. These were the consequences of choosing mortality. At first glance, mortality seems like something nobody would want to experience.

However, Eve saw it quite differently, saying, "Were it not for our transgression we never should have had seed, and never should have known good and evil, and the joy of our redemption, and the eternal life which God giveth unto all the obedient" (Moses 5:11). Part of mortality is experiencing opposites. Yes, there was sadness, but because there was sadness, there was also happiness. With the bad came the good. You cannot have one without the other. Could someone say they were righteous if they never had a chance to be wicked? Although the consequences of the Fall were painful, they also allowed progression.

The conditions we experience here allow us to learn and grow, even if that means making mistakes. Because of the promise of redemption through Jesus, even the wrong choices we make are not damning but rather developmental. As you and I stand over the graves of those we love, or worry about the consequences of sin, or experience the heartbreak of mortality, perhaps we can remember the wise perspective of Mother Eve. No, we do not like any of the hard parts of mortal life, but we would not choose any other way. It is through overcoming the hard that we experience what we actually came to do. To become. —DB

Reflect and Respond

How have some of the difficult parts of life on earth become an opportunity to experience the good?

Your favorite scripture in
Moses 5

MOSES 6:26

Enoch journeyed in the land.

One of the great contributions of Restoration scripture is the story of Enoch. In the book of Genesis, there are just a few verses that introduce, tell, and conclude his story. "And all the days of Enoch were three hundred sixty and five years: and Enoch walked with God: and he was not; for God took him" (Genesis 5:23–24). That's about it.

In contrast, in the book of Moses, the Lord revealed through Joseph Smith more than 115 verses that catalog the same story in much more exciting detail. They include Enoch's vast visions of the history of the earth from the beginning to the end, his recorded conversations with God, and the story of his great city being translated and taken into heaven, where they will wait until a magnificent return at the Second Coming of Christ. Those three hundred sixty and five years written about in the book of Genesis were no typical years. That is usually the case with everyone's life on earth, no matter the number of years they are here. In that great telling of Enoch's story in the book of Moses, we find this verse: "Enoch journeyed in the land . . . and as he journeyed, the Spirit of God descended out of heaven, and abode upon him" (Moses 6:26).

Everything Enoch experienced and learned came during his journey. It is how all of us experience and learn. It is on the journey that we gain our vision. It is on the journey that we have our most intimate conversations with God. And it is on the journey that we become closer to Him and anxiously await His coming. We learn all these things best when we are on the journey. —DB

Reflect and Respond

What are some of the great lessons and experiences you have had as you have journeyed?

Your favorite scripture in **Moses 6**

MOSES 7:21

**He beheld, and lo, Zion, in process of time,
was taken up into heaven.**

Some of the most difficult and stressful decisions Jenny and I have ever made have been deciding where we want to live. Picking a house and a neighborhood is a straight gamble. You want to find people you will like, a house you can grow into, and location, location, location is golden, of course. If ever in the history of the world there was a place that would make that decision a piece of cake, it would be moving to Zion, the city of Enoch—a city with people who were so good, they were eventually taken into God's rest. It was a city that was described as being a place where the people lived in righteousness, with one heart and one mind, and with no poor among them. They loved and took care of each other well. This description is one that delighted Joseph Smith, and it became a constant ambition of his to re-create it.

Perhaps Zion is something that you are seeking to re-create within your own home, family, and community. If so, Enoch's city offers two lessons that might give you encouragement. First, it should be noted that the city of Enoch grew up in a world that was soaked with wickedness, one that not many years later would be flooded in consequence.

Like many prophets, Enoch was shown an expansive vision of the history of the world. There are so many scenes in the past that I would love to be able to watch. There are others that I think I would want to close my eyes for. So much has happened throughout history that is so unsettling. I have met many people who have questioned the existence of God and His character after they have lived through or heard of some of the tragedies that happen around them. Many of them wondered if God actually cared.

During Enoch's vision, he saw the devil holding a great chain in his hands as he veiled the earth with darkness, and he heard him laugh with his unholy angels. I don't imagine Enoch could ever unhear that evil sound. As he turned to the Lord, he saw something that surprised him. God was weeping. As God looked down upon the earth, it was with tears in His eyes. Enoch was surprised. He asked, "How is it that thou canst weep?"

(Moses 7:29). God's simple response: "These thy brethren; they are the workmanship of mine own hands" (Moses 7:32).

We live in a world that is at times veiled with darkness, and we can almost hear the rattle of the devil's chains in the lives of those we love. Sometimes things are so heartbreaking, we are led to question God. We know His purposes and His wisdom are greater than all of ours combined, but there will still be times when we will be sad and confused. I suppose that is part of the journey. But in my wondering and unanswered questions, I find it helpful and encouraging to remember that we worship a God who weeps. Let's not forget, on the days we can't see His hand, that we know what His heart is like. Because I know that God cares, I know that whatever my surroundings are, I can still experience and build Zion.

The second lesson: I love to read that it was "in process of time" that the city of Zion was built. That admirable unity, love, and righteousness came day by day—perhaps almost imperceptibly. One kind word here, a small sacrifice there, bit by bit, in process of time. That was how Zion was built. And that is exactly how Zion will be and is being built this very day. —DB

Reflect and Respond

What is one small thing you can do to contribute to a feeling of Zion in your home, community, or heart?

Your favorite scripture in **Moses 7**

GENESIS 6:22

Thus did Noah; **according to all that God commanded him**, so did he.

Noah lived in a time when people didn't do all that the Lord commanded. Those of his day were so wicked that "every imagination of the . . . heart was only evil continually" (Genesis 6:5). Except Noah's. Somehow Noah found grace with the Lord, and the state of his heart allowed him to walk with God. I believe that a walk with God would take place along a covenant path, and that it would be filled with conversation along the way. Counsel. Commandment.

Noah was charged with doing all that the Lord commanded him. "Make thee an ark of gopher wood," the Lord counseled (Genesis 6:14). And Noah did. Bring your sons, and your wife, and your sons' wives, He commanded. And Noah did. "And of every living thing of all flesh, two of every sort shalt thou bring into the ark, to keep them alive with thee" (Genesis 6:19). And Noah did.

It couldn't have been easy, building a space that would become a refuge. Talking your wife and kids into traveling in that structure when shipbuilding isn't your profession. Herding and corralling that many animals into one place. The Bible doesn't record how many times Noah wanted to give up. Instead, it tells us twice, "Noah did according unto all that the Lord commanded him" (Genesis 7:5).

Then, one day, it began to rain. "And the waters prevailed upon the earth an hundred and fifty days. . . . And the ark rested in the seventh month" (Genesis 7:24; 8:4). For the entirety of that journey, Noah and his family were kept safe in a place of refuge because Noah did according to all that God commanded him. —EBF

Reflect and Respond

How has keeping the commandments of the Lord led to refuge in your life?

Your favorite scripture in **Genesis 6**

ABRAHAM 2:15

And I took Sarai **. . . and
the souls that we had won.**

When the Lord appeared to Abraham, He told him that He had a purpose for him—to make him a minister and to bless his family. Abraham knew he would do well to listen to the voice of the Lord, so he prepared to leave Haran and begin the journey to Canaan. "And I took Sarai, whom I took to wife when I was in Ur, in Chaldea, and Lot, my brother's son, and all our substance that we had gathered, and the souls that we had won" (Abraham 2:15). I am so interested in the souls that they had won. What is the story there? Because it feels like we live in a time when souls need winning.

We come to better understand what it might look like to win a soul as we watch Abraham's story continue to unfold. For example, when Abraham and Lot reached their destination, they stood together and looked out over the land. Abraham did not want there to be any strife, he wanted to remain as brothers, so he told Lot, "If thou wilt take the left hand, then I will go to the right; or if thou depart to the right hand, then I will go to the left. And Lot lifted up his eyes, and beheld all the plain of Jordan, that it was well watered every where, . . . and Lot dwelled in the cities of the plain, and pitched his tent *toward Sodom*" (Genesis 13:9–10, 12; emphasis added). Abraham walked the length and breadth of the remaining land, and then he chose his land by faith and pitched his tent in Hebron and built an altar to the Lord.

These are our clues to Abraham's character—wary of strife, desiring brotherhood, led by the Lord, walking by faith, focused upon sacrifice and worship. We discover a man who possessed a heart won over by God. Perhaps that is the prerequisite for winning souls. —EBF

Reflect and Respond

What or who has enabled your soul to be won by the Lord?

Your favorite scripture in Abraham 2

GENESIS 14:14

**And when Abram heard that his brother was taken captive,
he armed his trained servants, born in his own house.**

You may be familiar with the pioneer story of the Willie and Martin handcart companies, who were trapped in a snowstorm on their journey to the Salt Lake Valley. When news of their predicament reached the Saints already settled in the valley, Brigham Young, President of the Church at that time, stood up in general conference and gave a single message sermon as a compassionate detour from his planned talk. His message was essentially, "Go out on the plains and rescue them." That message has always been the message of Jesus—to rescue.

I know and have read about many people whom I would describe as having rescuing hearts, people who remind me of the Saints who left conference to travel into the snow. Abraham was one of those. When he and Lot split up, you'll remember that Lot went into the city of Sodom. While he was living there, the king of Sodom went to war with a neighbor, and, as a consequence of the conflict, Lot was captured. A servant escaped and came running to Abraham with the news. I often wonder why the servant came to Abraham in a time of trouble. Maybe it was because he and Lot were family. But I like to think it was because the servant knew Abraham's heart. Maybe he knew that Abraham was the type of man who would immediately gather his servants—servants who were already trained for rescue—and go out and pursue Lot until he had saved him. On that day, when the news came, he gathered 318 of his *own* servants, at his *own* expense, to save one single lost soul. A soul he thought was worth it. Abraham was a man who lived the message of Jesus: rescue. —DB

Reflect and Respond

When have you seen a rescuing heart in action?

Your favorite
scripture in
Genesis 14

GENESIS 17:2

**And I will make my covenant between me
and thee, and will multiply thee exceedingly.**

As you follow the story of the Bible, the first few pages of Genesis cover hundreds and hundreds of years of history. Then, suddenly, there is almost a screeching halt when we arrive at the story of the man Abraham. At that point, the narrative begins moving significantly slower. In Abraham's story, we are shown in greater detail than perhaps anywhere else in scripture the blessings, promises, and obligations of the covenant relationship that God enters into with His people. Perhaps all of the blessings could be summarized with the overarching promise that God would be their God, and they would be His people (see Genesis 17:7–8). As His people, they would then be heirs to all of the individual promises He made with Abraham, including a blessed land, posterity greater in number than the stars of the heavens, and access to the priesthood and gospel blessings (see Abraham 2:6, 11; 3:14). It would also be the posterity's privilege to take these same blessings to every nation and people of the world (see Abraham 1:19; 2:11).

When people talk about the Abrahamic covenant, they are referring to this collection of blessings, promises, and obligations that God made not only with Abraham and Sarah but also with their willing posterity (see Abraham 2:11). Each of these blessings seems to have an earthly fulfillment as well as a future heavenly one. As we read through them, we are left with an overwhelming sense of how good God was, how good God is, and how good He intends to be forever. Surely, as He said to Abraham, He would also say to us, "I will make my covenant between me and thee, and will multiply thee exceedingly" (Genesis 17:2). —DB

Reflect and Respond
Which blessings of the Abrahamic covenant does your heart particularly yearn for?

Your favorite
scripture in
Genesis 17

GENESIS 18:14

Is any thing too hard for the Lord?

When three holy men appeared to Abraham on the plains of Mamre, he immediately realized these holy men had the power to change his life—to bless it. He was not going to let that opportunity pass him by, so he offered them hospitality: "Pass not away . . . let a little water, I pray you, be fetched, and wash your feet, and rest yourselves under the tree: And I will fetch a morsel of bread, and comfort ye your hearts. . . . And they said, So do, as thou hast said" (Genesis 18:3–5).

Consider the way in which Abraham performed their request. He "hastened into the tent unto Sarah, and said, Make ready quickly three measures of fine meal . . . and Abraham ran unto the herd, and fetcht a calf . . . and he hasted to dress it . . . and he stood by them under the tree, and they did eat" (Genesis 18:6–8). His response causes me to ponder the way in which I go and do what the holy men in my life have asked of me, the apostles and prophets of our day—in my home, in my service, in my life. Do I hasten to perform their counsel? Do I quickly respond? In a world that mocks and questions, do I stand by them?

Abraham and Sarah's choice to follow these holy men led to a miraculous blessing in their life, one that could not have been realized without intervention from the Lord. What miraculous blessing does the Lord hold in store for you? In the moments when our hearts need comfort, let us remember to hasten to follow holy men quickly, knowing they will lead us closer to the One who will bring the miracles—that which He has spoken. "Is any thing too hard for the Lord?" (Genesis 18:14). —EBF

Reflect and Respond

How has following the prophet enabled the Lord to perform miracles in your life?

Your favorite scripture in **Genesis 18**

GENESIS 19:17

Look not behind thee.

Despite the reputation Sodom and Gomorrah had for being a terribly wicked place, Lot still decided to move himself and his family into the city. Whatever warnings there may have been, or whatever counsel Lot may have ignored, the Lord still sent messengers to his home to rescue and warn him about a pending destruction of the city. His instructions were clear: "Get you out of this place; . . . escape for thy life; look not behind thee" (Genesis 19:14, 17). With what seems like a hesitant exit, Lot and his family barely escaped the destruction. But as they were leaving, Lot's wife looked back, and she became a pillar of salt.

It's hard to know exactly what happened to her. Perhaps it happened just as it said—she literally turned to salt. Or perhaps she went back into the city and died by fire and brimstone. But whatever happened, one thing seems clear—she went against the warnings of the Lord. We may never know all the reasons why she turned back, but it is important to know that she didn't have to. The Lord had given her another option—an escape. Her past did not have to define her future.

Sometimes I read the Lord's "warning" as an encouragement. You don't *have* to look back at that place anymore. You can leave it in the past. Your journey is ahead of you, and it is better than where you came from. Sadly, Lot's wife may never have considered that what was ahead of her could be better than what she was leaving behind. As Elder Jeffrey R. Holland once said, "Faith is for the future. Faith builds on the past but never longs to stay there. Faith trusts that God has great things in store for each of us and that Christ truly is the 'high priest of good things to come.'"[2] —DB

Reflect and Respond

What is a future hope or blessing that is encouraging you to move forward in your life?

Your favorite scripture in **Genesis 19**

GENESIS 21:17

**Fear not; for God hath heard
the voice of the lad where he is.**

It is hard to know from what is written in the Bible what actually happened between Sarah and Hagar or perhaps even between their sons, Isaac and Ishmael, but somehow there was anger and contention in the family of Abraham. The problem was between the two women, and the solution, as sad as it was, was to send Hagar and her son, Ishmael, out into the wilderness.

Abraham sent them with provisions of food and water, but they didn't last long enough. Soon, Hagar found herself destitute, placing her dying boy under a shrub. Then, she went off alone to cry. I cannot imagine the pain and heartache of her soul in the moment when it looked like all was lost. All she had left to do was pray. "And God heard . . ." (Genesis 21:17). As she was pleading, He was listening. God heard her prayer and sent an angel with these comforting words: "Fear not; for God hath heard the voice of the lad where he is" (Genesis 21:17).

It is easy in wilderness places to feel like God has forgotten about us or perhaps doesn't even know where we are. Hagar was, after all, one single woman—an outcast crying in the barren land. Just as His eye was on Abraham and Sarah and Isaac, so too was it on her. He had not forgotten her. Before He opened her eyes to see a well of water waiting for her—perhaps prepared for her before she ever got there—He first reassured her of that. Before He gave her the drink she so desperately needed, He gave her the truth she perhaps needed more: *"God hath heard the voice of the lad where he is . . ."* He knew where they were. He knew their story and their hearts. He knew exactly what they needed, and He was there to provide. —DB

Reflect and Respond
When has God let you know that He knows exactly where you are?

Your favorite scripture in
Genesis 21

GENESIS 22:17

In blessing I will bless thee.

As I consider the journey that took place on the road to Moriah, I ponder the thoughts that must have filled Abraham's heavy heart. "Take now thy son, thine only son Isaac, whom thou lovest" (Genesis 22:2). I imagine the sun rising early that morning, the gathering of the wood, the planning for the three-day journey ahead. I think of the thoughts that must have filled Abraham's heart every time he lifted his eyes to see the place afar off. I imagine the last stretch of that journey, as Abraham climbed the mountain with his son—his only son, whom he loved. When he came to the place God had told him of, I picture him building the altar somberly with his own hands and carefully laying out the wood, each piece in order. It is beyond my capacity to understand what he must have felt as he gently bound his trusting, obedient son and laid him on the altar.

And then, when Abraham stretched forth his hand, an angel called unto him—in the very moment when it became clear that Abraham would not withhold anything from the Lord. When asked why God commanded Abraham to sacrifice Isaac, President Hugh B. Brown suggested it was because "Abraham needed to learn something about Abraham."[3] I wonder, What do I need to learn about myself? What am I willing to give to the Lord to learn that lesson? What am I willing to sacrifice?

After reading about Abraham, I realize that I must become more willing to take the journey, to climb the mountain, to withhold nothing—even when I don't know what the end of the path will bring. As Susan Tanner wrote: "Each time I walk with Abraham and Isaac on the road to Mount Moriah, I weep, knowing that Abraham does not know that there will be an angel and a ram in the thicket at the end of the journey. We are each in the middle of our earthly path, and we don't know the rest of our own stories. But we, as Abraham, are blessed with miracles."[4]

The road to Moriah is a road filled with sacrifice. But it is also a road filled with miracles. A favorite hymn reminds me, "Sacrifice brings forth the blessings of heaven."[5] I think of Abraham, and my heart knows the truth of that phrase.

As Abraham and Isaac prepared to leave Mount Moriah, the angel called unto Abraham a second time, saying, "Because thou hast done this thing, and hast not withheld thy son, thine only son: that in blessing I will bless thee . . . because thou hast obeyed my voice" (Genesis 22:16–18).

What does your sacrifice look like?

What are the stones you lift every day?

What is the bundle of wood you carry?

In the Mount Moriah moments of our lives, in the moments when we choose to withhold nothing from the Lord, in the moments of greatest sacrifice, perhaps we could try to remember that in His own way and in His own time, the Lord will provide the angel and the ram in the thicket. When all is said and done, He will withhold nothing from us. In blessing He will bless us. May our eyes be open to recognize those blessings. —EBF

Reflect and Respond

What are you willing to sacrifice to know the Lord?

Your favorite scripture in Genesis 22

GENESIS 24:67

. . . and he loved her.

One of the best love stories in the scriptures is found in the twenty-fourth chapter of Genesis. First let me introduce you to Rebekah, a damsel with a kind heart, "And the servant ran to meet her, and said, Let me, I pray thee, drink a little water of thy pitcher. And she said, Drink, my lord: and she hasted, and let down her pitcher upon her hand, and gave him drink. And when she had done giving him drink, she said, *I will draw water for thy camels also, until they have done drinking*" (Genesis 24:17–19; emphasis added). Do you know how much a camel can drink? Up to twenty gallons in one sitting. Out of the goodness of her heart, Rebekah offered to draw water for the servant's camels with her pitcher—*until they were done drinking.*

This kind damsel is about to be introduced to Isaac—a boy who was loved much, who was obedient, who was trustworthy. "Isaac went out to meditate in the field at the eventide: and he lifted up his eyes, and saw, and, behold, the camels were coming. And Rebekah lifted up her eyes, and when she saw Isaac, she lighted off the camel. For she had said unto the servant, What man is this that walketh in the field to meet us?" (Genesis 24:63–65). At this point in the story, the details become a little sparse. We don't get to read about the introduction, or the courtship, or the details of the wedding, but we do know this: "She became his wife; and he loved her" (Genesis 24:67). Three simple words that evoke powerful emotion: *He loved her.*

I find so much joy knowing that Isaac loved Rebekah, the damsel with the kind heart.

It's a love story that makes me happy. A fairy tale filled with adventure and romance, courage and hope, and everlasting love. —EBF

Reflect and Respond

What part does kindness play in love?

Your favorite scripture in
Genesis 24

GENESIS 25:22

And she went to inquire of the Lord.

The entire story of Jacob began with a struggle. Isaac and Rebekah had waited long for a child, but eventually, by the grace of God, she found herself expecting twins. Sometime during the pregnancy, she noticed that "the children struggled together within her" (Genesis 25:22). In a way that her unborn sons would eventually need to learn, when a problem came into Rebekah's life, "she went to inquire of the Lord" (Genesis 25:22). She looked to God for strength and wisdom, and He taught her and encouraged her about her sons' future.

Esau was born first, but he came into the world with Jacob, his younger twin, holding on to his heel. Jacob's name in Hebrew seems to be a play on words that either means "heel" or the word for "supplanter, deceiver, or one who overreaches." Certainly these words don't describe Jacob's full character, but at times he seemed to live up to the second name. Remember the day Esau came home from the fields apparently starving to the point of near death? He found Jacob making lentil pottage and begged him for food. Jacob took advantage of the situation and asked his brother to sell his birthright in exchange for a bowl—which Esau did. Perhaps Esau did not value his birthright the way he should, but perhaps Jacob should have taken care of his hungry brother instead of taking advantage of him. Throughout the brothers' lives, there was tension and deceit between them. Unlike their mother, the boys dealt with their struggles in ways that would lead to even more problems. Their story seems to show us the difference between looking to God for help and taking matters into your own hands. —DB

Reflect and Respond

When have you felt led to inquire of the Lord? Did you? Or did you take matters into your own hands?

Your favorite scripture in **Genesis 25**

GENESIS 27:36

For he hath supplanted me these two times . . .

In a very intense moment of a high school basketball game, just after a turnover, my daughter's coach called for a time out. He waited until he had the complete focus of the five players who had come off the floor, and then he said, "I'm not worried about you making mistakes. I know you are going to make mistakes. It's what you do after the mistake that I care about. It's how you recover." I watched that moment from the stands and knew I had just been taught a lesson that was as true in life as in basketball. The moments after the mistakes, the ways in which we recover, can often become the defining moments of our lives.

The entire story of Jacob is a lesson on making mistakes and learning how to recover. Jacob's biggest mistake was that he wanted to rely on his own devices to fulfill God's plan for his life. "Such hours come to most of us, when it almost seems as if necessity obliged and holy wisdom prompted us to accomplish, in our own strength, that which, nevertheless, we should leave in God's hand. . . . Here faith is the only true remedy: faith, which leaves God to carry out His own purposes, content to trust Him absolutely, and to follow Him whithersoever He leadeth. . . . God's way is never through the thicket of cunning and devices."[6]

The story of Jacob teaches us the importance of letting the Lord lead, of being patient, rather than trying to control our destiny by our own strength. Like Jacob, each of us will make mistakes. What the Lord watches for is what we do after that mistake—how we recover. In those defining moments, will we be willing to wrestle with the Savior? Will we allow the Lord to change us for good? Will we let God prevail? —EBF

Reflect and Respond

When is a time you have allowed the Lord to prevail in your life?

Your favorite scripture in Genesis 27

GENESIS 28:15

**For I will not leave thee, until I have done
that which I have spoken to thee of.**

When Jacob left his home and family, it was on unsettling terms. Esau was enraged with him after Jacob deceived him and his father. Rebekah, his mother, feared for his life and pleaded with him to go to her own father's land until things hopefully blew over. On his way, he found himself one night in an unnamed desert place where he was forced to sleep with rocks as his pillows. Perhaps he wondered how he had gotten into such a hopeless situation—a fugitive from home, with severed family relationships and no inkling of what the future held.

As he slept, he dreamed a dream. In it, he saw a ladder with angels going up and down. He also saw the Lord, standing above or beside him, and heard Him promise Jacob of a glorious potential and future, promises similar to the ones the Lord made with Abraham, his grandfather, and Isaac, his father. The Lord then promised Jacob His continual presence on his journey. "I am with thee, and will keep thee in all places whither thou goest, . . . for I will not leave thee, until I have done that which I have spoken to thee of" (Genesis 28:15).

When Jacob woke up, I imagine he was surprised that the Lord would have met him in a place like that. *In this place? In this unnamed desert with rocks for pillows and all of the trouble I brought upon myself?* Yes, Jacob, in this place.

The Lord meets us where we are, no matter what the situation may look like—even if we are the ones who got ourselves there. And when He comes, He brings ladders, angels, and promises, including the reassurance that He will walk with us in our journey wherever we go until He eventually fulfills every promise. He will not leave us until He has. —DB

Reflect and Respond

When have you experienced the love and presence of God in an unexpected place?

Your favorite
scripture in
Genesis 28

GENESIS 29:35

Now will I praise the Lord.

My heart aches for Leah. When Jacob arrived in Haran, he was immediately struck with the beauty of her younger sister, Rachel. The scriptures describe Leah as "tender eyed," which evidently was not a compliment. It took deceit for her father to marry her to Jacob, and I cannot imagine how her heart must have ached at Jacob's anger when he realized he had not married Rachel, but Leah instead. Do you wonder how she felt when he expressed his dissatisfaction with Leah and was willing to work even longer for a chance to still marry her younger sister?

Perhaps we get a peek into her sorrow by the way she named her children. Her first-born was named Reuben, a name that means, "Look, a son!" Maybe she thought that if she gave Jacob a son, he would actually love her. *Look, Jacob, a son!* It didn't seem to work, because she was still hated. She named her next son Simeon, which means "to be heard." Perhaps Jacob would listen to her now—notice her. The next boy was named Levi, a name that means "joined or pledged." "Now," she said, "this time will my husband be joined unto me" (Genesis 29:34).

Leah seemed desperate for love, acceptance, meaning, and purpose. She tried to find it in her marriage and with her children but was left wanting. However, Leah seemed to learn an important lesson sometime between her third and fourth son. When that fourth son was born, she didn't mention the love or acceptance of Jacob, but rather exclaimed, "Now will I praise the Lord" (Genesis 29:35). *Now I will look to Him for my love, acceptance, meaning, and purpose.* And she named that son Judah, which means "to praise the Lord." —DB

Reflect and Respond

How does looking to the Lord for love and acceptance satisfy your soul in ways that nothing else can?

Your favorite scripture in **Genesis 29**

GENESIS 32:28

**Thy name shall be called no more Jacob, but Israel:
for as a prince hast thou power with God and with men.**

Someone once told me that the best way to help someone change is by giving them a new identity. A person tends to act like the person they believe they are. Jacob's journey began with and continued to be a struggle, but God did not give up on him, just like He promised He wouldn't (see Genesis 28:15).

There is a beautiful moment in Jacob's story, when he is about to meet up with his brother, Esau, that shows the change of heart Jacob has experienced. Unlike his typical way of approaching problems, when Jacob heard that Esau was coming (the same Esau he fled from because of his lies and deceit), instead of arranging a trick or swindle, Jacob turned to the Lord in prayer. "O God of my father Abraham, . . . I am not worthy of the least of all the mercies. . . . Deliver me, I pray thee" (Genesis 32:9–11). That night, Jacob wrestled all through the night with a holy being. Perhaps the wrestle was an indication of his own wrestle in his soul. When the morning came, Jacob asked for a blessing. The holy visitor asked him, "What is thy name? And he said, Jacob. And he said, Thy name shall be called no more Jacob, but Israel" (Genesis 32:27–28). Israel is a name that means "he perseveres, or prevails, with God." For so long, Jacob had tried to do things on his own, but now he was different. Now he would prevail, not because of his own wit, but because of the strength of God. —DB

Reflect and Respond

Why is it such a wrestle to allow God to take over in our lives?

Your favorite
scripture in
Genesis 32

GENESIS 33:11

. . . because God hath dealt graciously with me,
and because I have enough . . .

When the Lord told Jacob to return to his own country and to his family and promised that all would be well, Jacob was nervous and pleaded, "Deliver me, I pray thee, from the hand of my brother, from the hand of Esau: for I fear him" (Genesis 32:11). But Jacob had learned to allow the Lord to prevail in his life, so he went.

On that day, when Jacob was almost home, he saw Esau coming with four hundred men, and again fear filled his heart. Jacob worried for his family. But Esau ran to meet him, "and fell on his neck, and kissed him: and they wept" (Genesis 33:4). Jacob tried to offer gifts to Esau, presents meant to find grace in his sight, but Esau said, "I have enough, my brother; keep that thou hast unto thyself." Jacob refused, saying, "Take . . . my blessing that is brought to thee; because God hath dealt graciously with me, and because I have enough" (Genesis 33:9, 11).

Perhaps that is where grace begins, in the surety of knowledge that God has cared so well for each of us that we have enough. Then giving grace becomes not only a response of gratitude to God but also a condition of the heart, because when we have experienced His gracious love, we can't help but extend the same to another.

The story that began with fighting in the womb, scarcity, deceit, selfishness, and greed ended with two brothers reconciled and willing to care for one another tenderly and softly. It is a beautiful story of giving grace.

What caused the change of heart for both brothers?

Three simple words: *I have enough.* —EBF

Reflect and Respond
When has God dealt graciously with you?

Your favorite scripture in **Genesis 33**

GENESIS 35:15

**And Jacob called the name of the place
where God spake with him, Beth-el.**

Emily and I once told the story of Jacob's journey to a group of inmates in a prison. When we talked about that desert place where he found himself while he ran from his mistakes and from his brother, we emphasized how powerful it was that God still showed up for him there. We also spoke of how surprised Jacob was that he would ever find God in a place like that. One prisoner in the back of the classroom interrupted us with a raised hand and said, with tears in his eyes, "Probably the same way I was surprised to find God in a place like this."

After Jacob's experience, he named that once unnamed place "Bethel," a name that means "the house of God." It probably didn't look like a house of God—but because God had come to Jacob there, that ordinary place became beautiful and holy. The same way the prison did to our friend we met there.

Later in his life, the Lord wanted Jacob to return to Bethel. So Jacob prepared all of his household and took them on a journey to "the place where God spake with him." There, Jacob told them the story and perhaps explained why it was such a beautiful place in his eyes. Then the Lord renewed with Jacob those same promises He had made before.

I believe in a God who still meets us in ordinary places and turns them into holy places and memories. I believe these are stories He wants us to pass on so others can continually hope for and believe in a God who turns the ordinary into holy. —DB

Reflect and Respond

What is your Bethel? When has God turned ordinary into holy for you?

Your favorite scripture in **Genesis 35**

GENESIS 37:13

And he said to him,
Here am I.

Have you ever tried typing on an old-fashioned typewriter? It takes practice to press the key with just enough strength that it hits the ribbon and leaves its mark upon the paper waiting there. The inky letter that remains on that piece of paper is called a "type" or an impression of the true key itself.

The word *type* comes from the Greek *tupos,* which means "impression," and from *tuptein,* which means "to strike." *To strike an impression.* Sometimes in the scriptures we find a type, a symbol or representation, of another event. In the Book of Mormon, Mosiah speaks of things that were "types of things to come" (Mosiah 13:31).

Joseph of Egypt is often referred to as a type of Christ. Alfred Edersheim, a Bible scholar, wrote, "We cannot fail to recognize that although Joseph is not personally mentioned in the New Testament as a type of Christ, his history was eminently typical of that of our blessed Saviour, alike in *his betrayal, his elevation to highest dignity,* and his *preserving the life of his people,* and in *their ultimate recognition of him and repentance* of their sin."[7]

This time, as you read the story of Joseph, try to find examples of how he is a "type" of Christ, looking for Edersheim's four types to start with. How does his story *strike an impression* of the Savior's story? What other "types" might we find if we open our eyes to see them? You might look at the moment when Israel wanted Joseph to see whether it was well with his brothers and he replied, "Here am I" (Genesis 37:13).

What else will you discover? —EBF

Reflect and Respond
What is your favorite example of Joseph as a type of Christ?

Your favorite scripture in **Genesis 37**

GENESIS 38:26

She hath been more righteous than I.

Right in the middle of the story of Joseph, we read the story of Tamar. Some Bible scholars believe that her story was not placed here by accident; instead, it is an important reminder that God can right the wrongs of others and restore promises that have been withheld.

In this chapter, Judah, the older brother of Joseph, is depicted as a selfish man who withholds his promise. Tamar is his daughter-in-law, married to his oldest son, Er. Shortly into the marriage we discover Er is a wicked man, and the Lord slays him (see Genesis 38:7). When he dies, Judah gives Tamar to his second son, Onan, according to the custom of levirate marriage. Onan does not want any children from Tamar. He knows the birthright will be passed to that child along with his share of the inheritance. God punishes him for his behavior by death. Perhaps refusing to see the wickedness in his sons and believing Tamar is dangerous, Judah becomes unwilling to keep his responsibility to give her to his third son. He sends her back to her family to live out her life as a widow.

After waiting in vain for Judah to fulfill his promise according to the levirate custom, Tamar feels prompted to take action. She covers her face and stands at the side of the road waiting for Judah, who is now also a widower, to pass by. Driven by personal gratification, Judah uses Tamar for his own pleasure. As she leaves, Tamar asks Judah, "What wilt thou give me . . . ?" (Genesis 38:16). Judah offers her a goat, and, as a pledge that he will give that payment, he gives Tamar his signet, cord, and staff.

In time, the city realizes Tamar is with child. After finding out, Judah wants to put her to death until she pulls out his signet. In that moment he acknowledges his failure in the situation saying, "she hath been more righteous than I" (Genesis 38:26).

This experience becomes a turning point for Judah. But this story is also an important reminder for each of us as we enter back into the story of Joseph. There will be people who will wrong us in this life. Things will be taken from us. Promises will be withheld. We might be led into situations we wouldn't choose, but the Lord can right those wrongs.

He did it for Tamar, and we are about to watch Him perform those miracles again in Joseph's story. God will restore promises that have been withheld. In time He will recompense us, and all of the wrongs will be made right.

You might find it interesting to note that it is through the line of Tamar's twins that Jesus will be born (see Matthew 1:3). This woman was one of His great-grandmothers. Sometimes I like to remind myself that where He came from became a witness of who He came for. —EBF

Reflect and Respond

When has the Lord righted a wrong in your life?

Your favorite scripture in
Genesis 38

GENESIS 39:21

But the Lord was with Joseph . . .

If you were to look at Joseph's life from the outside, you might not consider it very ideal. After he was thrown into a pit and sold off to a traveling caravan by his own brothers, he was taken to Egypt, where he was sold again to a man named Potiphar as a servant in his household. But the Lord was with him, and he prospered even as a servant. Potiphar could see there was something unique about Joseph, so he made him the overseer of his entire household, and the Lord blessed Joseph and the household of Potiphar.

But trouble came again. The wife of Potiphar became infatuated with Joseph and wanted him for herself. Joseph refused, but Potiphar's wife continued to press him day after day. Joseph remained steadfast in his honor and virtue. One day, as Joseph was doing his work, Potiphar's wife grabbed onto his clothes and pulled him in to "lie with" her (Genesis 39:12). But Joseph broke free and ran away. Angry with his resistance, or perhaps embarrassed and nervous about what he would do, Potiphar's wife accused Joseph of attacking her, and soon Joseph was thrown into the king's prison for crimes he did not commit.

Now he was a prisoner. All that he had worked for was lost. But the Lord was still with him. Soon, the keeper of the prison noticed something unique about him, began to trust him, and put him in charge of the other prisoners. He began to prosper even as a prisoner, just as he had as a slave and a servant. Whatever happened to Joseph, things seemed to still turn out. Because the Lord was with him, he was able to find grace and prosperity in any of the situations he was put into. —DB

Reflect and Respond

When have you found grace and prosperity in less-than-ideal situations?

Your favorite scripture in
Genesis 39

GENESIS 41:16

**It is not in me: God shall
give Pharaoh an answer of peace.**

The pharaoh of Egypt was having troubling dreams. He dreamt he was standing by a river and saw seven healthy cows feeding in the meadows. Soon, seven skinny, malnourished cows came and swallowed up the seven healthy ones. That bizarre dream was followed by another one. This time he dreamt about seven ears of corn that grew on a single stalk. They were bright and healthy looking. Then a wind came, and seven thin, crackling ears of corn grew up and devoured the healthy corn, just as had happened with the cows in his other dream.

When he woke up, he called in all of his magicians and dream interpreters to help him understand what he was experiencing. None of them could help. As Pharaoh's butler observed what was happening, he had a sudden stroke of memory. When he was in prison after the pharaoh had been upset with him, he and a fellow prisoner had also had dreams they couldn't figure out. There was another prisoner who had interpreted both of their dreams correctly. That prisoner was Joseph. The pharaoh sent immediately for him.

As he questioned Joseph about his ability to interpret dreams, Joseph humbly replied, "It is not in me: God shall give Pharaoh an answer of peace" (Genesis 41:16). In other words, *I cannot interpret dreams, but God can. I cannot bring you peace or help you in the way you would like—but I know Someone who will.* With Joseph as His servant and instrument, God interpreted the dreams of Pharaoh. Seven years of plenty were coming, and they were going to be followed by seven years of famine. The dream was a warning. Through Joseph, God blessed and preserved the nation of Egypt in a way no one else could. —DB

Reflect and Respond

When has God blessed you through someone else? Or when have you been God's instrument?

Your favorite scripture in
Genesis 41

GENESIS 42:35

. . . as they emptied their sacks . . .

Have you ever noticed what happened every time Joseph's brothers left him in Egypt to return to their father? The first time, they stopped at an inn, "and it came to pass as they emptied their sacks, that, behold, every man's bundle of money was in his sack" (Genesis 42:35).

When they returned to Joseph the second time they explained that they had found the money in their sacks, "and we have brought it again in our hand. And other money have we brought down in our hands to buy food: we cannot tell who put our money in our sacks." And Joseph replied, "Peace be to you, fear not: your God, and the God of your father, hath given you treasure in your sacks" (Genesis 43:21–23). As they prepared to leave for home the second time, Joseph commanded his steward to "fill the men's sacks with food, as much as they can carry, and put every man's money in his sack's mouth" (Genesis 44:1). He gave them not just enough to supply their needs, but more. Much more.

The third time the brothers left, a sack was not sufficient. This time Joseph sent wagons and horses laden with food and other good things. If Joseph is a type of Christ, then we have just been taught a very important characteristic of the Lord—He gives not just enough to simply supply our needs, but more. Much more.

My mind is focused on the image of ten brothers who, as they emptied their sacks, discovered treasure beyond their expectations. What might we discover if we were to figuratively empty our sacks to make room for the treasure the Lord has for us? We'll likely find spiritual gifts beyond our expectations. Sacks filled with treasure. As much as we can carry. —EBF

Reflect and Respond
What gifts beyond expectation has the Lord given you?

Your favorite scripture in **Genesis 42**

GENESIS 50:19

Am I in the place of God?

In the moment when Joseph's brothers came pleading, in the moment when they asked forgiveness for the great trial they had imposed upon him, just when he could have turned to them and said, "Why the pit, why the bag of silver in place of a brother, why the years in prison?" instead he asked them a profound question: "For am I in the place of God?" (Genesis 50:19). It was as if he were saying, "In the end, isn't the place where I ended up after all those trials the exact place God needed me to be?" *Am I not in the place God designed?* Think about it. Had there not been the pit, the slavery, the years in prison, there would not have been the opportunity for leadership, for preserving a nation, for saving his family. The truth of it is, the trial was what enabled him to be in the place he needed to be. *The place God needed him to be.* I love this line, "As for you, ye thought evil against me; but God meant it unto good, to bring to pass, as it is this day, to save much people alive" (Genesis 50:20).

What a profound message! Joseph experienced a trial that had the potential to destroy him, but God meant it unto good. God *turned it* unto good.

Think of the greatest trial in your life. Can you see how God meant it unto you for good? If you can't see it now, ask that He will open your heart to understand. In the midst of our greatest trials, it's okay to question. We just have to make sure we are asking the right question. Asking "why" might not help us discover the answer we are truly seeking. Perhaps the right question to ask in the midst of tribulation is the one Joseph asked, "Am I in the place of God?" *Is this trial helping me to arrive at the place God needs me to be?*—EBF

Reflect and Respond

How is a current trial helping you to arrive at the place God needs you to be?

Your favorite scripture in Genesis 50

EXODUS 1:17

**But the midwives feared God, and did not as the king of Egypt
commanded them, but saved the men children alive.**

When the rest of the family of Jacob moved into Egypt with Joseph, they were in total about seventy people, but soon their numbers began to increase exponentially. As time passed, a new leader came into power in the land of Egypt who did not know Joseph or the story of the Israelite people. He was threatened with how large and influential they were growing. Perhaps afraid they would one day rise up and take over his kingdom, the new leader made the Israelites slaves. He burdened them with building his treasure cities, but the more he tried to afflict them, the larger and stronger they grew. He attempted to make their lives miserable with difficult tasks and to crush their spirits and growing numbers, but it didn't work.

In a new tactic, the king gathered the Hebrew midwives and commanded them that when a baby was born, if it was a boy, they were to kill it immediately. But the midwives knew this was wrong, and they disobeyed the king, even at the risk of their own peril. They loved and honored God and what was right more than they cared for their own lives. The king of Egypt was powerful, ruthless, and certainly influential, but these courageous women served another King.

You cannot help but wonder how many lives they spared and how many hearts were healed because of the stand they took against what was wrong. They made a difference in the story, and God honored these women for the noble work they were quietly doing. They set the stage for the beautiful beginning of a story of deliverance. —DB

Reflect and Respond

When have you seen courage and bravery in honoring the will of God?

Your favorite
scripture in
Exodus 1

EXODUS 2:25

And God looked upon the children of Israel . . .

A snapshot of the children of Israel in Egypt might tempt you to believe that God had forgotten about them. Their lives were miserable. Sunup to sundown they were working as slaves, crying for deliverance. But deliverance was on its way. Within the families of the Israelites there was a baby boy born to a Levite couple. Pharaoh had a law that all newborn boys were to be killed, so this new mother hid her baby as long as she could. When she could no longer keep him a secret, no doubt under the inspiration of heaven, she made a little ark from the bulrushes, put her precious baby inside, and sent him forth into the river with a prayer.

Despite everything that could certainly go wrong with a baby floating down a river, the ark miraculously found its way to the spot where Pharaoh's daughter went down to wash in the river. Compassion melted her heart when she opened the ark and saw the baby—even though he was Hebrew and her own father had given the death sentence. That little baby boy, whom she named Moses, grew up as a son to Pharaoh's daughter until a fateful day when he defended one of his Hebrew brethren and an Egyptian guard died. He was forced to escape as a fugitive, but once more miraculously ran into a family at just the right time who would prove to be instrumental in his future mission.

As Moses continued to learn and grow in his new home, the children of Israel continued to cry for deliverance. Perhaps they thought they were forgotten. But God had His eye upon them. Through the work of a floating ark, an inspired mother, a courageous princess, an assisted escape, and a place prepared for refuge, Israel's deliverance was already in motion. —DB

Reflect and Respond
When have you looked back and seen God orchestrating goodness in your life?

Your favorite scripture in Exodus 2

EXODUS 3:5

Put off thy shoes from off thy feet.

Early in the book of Exodus we read the story of Moses and the burning bush. "And the angel of the Lord appeared unto him in a flame of fire out of the midst of a bush: and he looked, and, behold, the bush burned with fire, and the bush was not consumed. And Moses said, *I will now turn aside, and see this great sight,* why the bush is not burnt. And when the Lord saw that he *turned aside to see,* God called unto him out of the midst of the bush, and said, Moses, Moses. And he said, Here am I. And he said, Draw not nigh hither: *put off thy shoes from off thy feet,* for the place whereon thou standest is holy ground" (Exodus 3:2–5; emphasis added).

Notice that it wasn't until after Moses turned aside to see the great sight that the place where he stood became holy unto him. He stopped what he was doing, laid aside the task he was focused on, and took a moment to notice the miracle in the midst of the mundane. *How do we learn to do that?* How can we find a way to stop what we are doing, lay aside the task we are focused on, and recognize the glory of God in the middle of the ordinary details of our day? If we could learn to do that, we too might discover holy moments in our midst. Elizabeth Barrett Browning said, "Every common bush [is] afire with God—but only he who sees takes off his shoes."[8] *Only he who sees.*

The Lord is everywhere. His mercies and His miracles surround us. Turn aside to see the great sight.

Take off your shoes. —EBF

Reflect and Respond
Where have you stood on holy ground?

Your favorite scripture in Exodus 3

EXODUS 7:5

And the Egyptians shall know that I am the Lord.

When Moses came to Pharaoh with the Lord's commandment to let His people go, Pharaoh responded by asking, "Who is the Lord, that I should obey his voice . . . ? I know not the Lord" (Exodus 5:2). If Pharaoh let his workforce go free, it seems it would severely cripple the Egyptian economy as well as Pharaoh's ego. It is not surprising that he would not let them go—especially since he did not know who was asking. He did not know the Lord. So the Lord began to showcase who He was, telling Moses, "And the Egyptians shall know that I am the Lord" (Exodus 7:5).

It began small, comparatively, with Aaron's staff being turned into a serpent in Pharaoh's court. Pharaoh was unimpressed, especially when his magicians could do the same thing. The next day, Moses put his staff into the river, and the rivers and lakes and bodies of water in Egypt were turned to blood. It was devastating to Egypt to be without water, but still Pharaoh refused to free the Israelites. But the Lord sent Moses again, and again and again, to Pharaoh, each time with a new plague that vexed the land. Frogs, lice, locusts, boils. And each time, Pharaoh would promise to let the people go if Moses would ask the Lord to reverse the plague. And when the Lord did, Pharaoh would reverse his promise. This happened ten times. Ten different plagues. Moses going back again and again at the command of the Lord.

The Lord was just as interested in saving Pharaoh as He was in saving Moses. The Lord loved the Egyptians with the same love He had for the Israelites. Pharaoh was hardening his heart, but the Lord was trying to win it. Perhaps that's why He gave so many chances. —DB

Reflect and Respond

When have you seen God's patience and love come through chastisement and chances?

Your favorite scripture in
Exodus 7

EXODUS 13:3

Remember this day.

Of all the plagues that came to Egypt, the last of them would be the most devastating. On a certain night, at midnight, every firstborn in all of Egypt would perish. *Every* firstborn. The people of Israel had been spared the effects of the previous plagues, but this one would impact everyone—from least to greatest. But there was a way to be delivered. The Lord instructed anyone who would listen how to avoid the plague, how to be passed over: Each household was to take a lamb that was a firstborn male, without blemish. They were to keep the lamb in their home for several days, until a given night, when they would kill the lamb in the evening and roast it for a meal. The blood of the lamb was to be taken and painted upon the upper and two side posts of the door. "And the blood shall be to you for a token upon the houses where ye are: and when I see the blood, I will pass over you, and the plague shall not be upon you" (Exodus 12:13).

And so it happened as the Lord said it would. In some homes, the firstborn perished, and a cry went up in the land. In other homes, a firstborn lamb was slain, and its blood marked the home, and the plague passed over them. In those homes, they knew deliverance came because the lamb had died in their place.

"And this day shall be unto you for a memorial" (Exodus 12:14). This was a moment the Lord wanted to make sure they never forgot. "Remember this day," He told them (Exodus 13:3). And this feast they would re-create each year and tell their children and their children's children the story of the day they were saved by the blood of the lamb. It would be their national story—what they were known by—a people saved by their God. —DB

....

Reflect and Respond
What miracle of God do you always want to remember?

Your favorite
scripture in
Exodus 13

EXODUS 14:13

**Fear ye not, stand still, and see
the salvation of the Lord.**

Can you imagine standing on the shore of the Red Sea? Sand to the right. Sand to the left. An ocean ahead of you. Imagine looking back and seeing the flood of Egyptians approaching behind you, hearing the horse's hooves and chariot wheels beat the drum of your execution.

Imagine being Moses. In that moment the multitude would glance at the water, and then all eyes would shift to him. They all looked to Moses "sore afraid" (Exodus 14:10).

Here is where Moses will win your heart. He will remember what Israel has so easily forgotten. "Fear ye not," he said, "stand still, and see the salvation of the Lord, which he will shew to you to day" (Exodus 14:13). *Don't you remember the frogs, the locusts, the lice? Have you forgotten the lambs, the blood upon doorposts, the deliverance?* And yet, in a moment of fear, the Israelites began to panic. "It had been better for us to serve the Egyptians," they say (Exodus 14:12). Elder Jeffrey R. Holland beautifully responds:

"How soon we forget. . . . Of course our faith will be tested as we fight through these self-doubts and second thoughts. Some days we will be miraculously led out of Egypt— seemingly free, seemingly on our way—only to come to yet another confrontation, like all that water lying before us. At those times we must resist the temptation to panic and to give up. At those times fear will be the strongest of the adversary's weapons against us. . . . Nobody had ever crossed the Red Sea this way before, but so what. There's always a first time. Dismiss your fear and wade in with both feet."[9] —DB

Reflect and Respond

How might standing still and looking to the Lord allow Him to work miracles in your behalf?

Your favorite scripture in Exodus 14

EXODUS 16:21

And they gathered it every morning . . .

The children of Israel prayed and pleaded for a deliverance from Egypt for years, but when it finally came, it had unanticipated surprises. They were in a new place with new challenges. One of those was eating. How would they find food in their new wilderness home? The situation was dire enough that within a short period of time after miraculously crossing through the Red Sea, the people of Israel began to panic about the lack of food—actually believing that they would die of starvation.

As they looked around, they saw no solution to the problem. But the Lord already had one prepared. As they journeyed, He would provide their food. It was a small, bread-like morsel that tasted like a wafer with honey. They called it manna, a Hebrew word that means "What is it?" It was a new food that came in the most unexpected and surprising way.

Each morning it came, and the instructions were to gather just enough for their needs for that particular day. No more, no less. The Lord could have rained down weekly and monthly portions of manna, but instead He seemed to be teaching the children of Israel the need to rely on Him anew each and every day.

There is wisdom, of course, in saving and storing up and planning ahead. But in this journey of life, we also learn how to rely upon the Lord day by day. He will provide for us exactly what we need for the day ahead. A daily miracle and reminder of a God who knows our daily needs. —DB

Reflect and Respond

As you look back on this day, where have you seen God provide for your needs?

Your favorite scripture in
Exodus 16

EXODUS 17:12

**Aaron and Hur stayed up his hands . . .
and his hands were steady.**

Part of the Israelites' journey through the wilderness included battles with other nations. We do not get many details, but one day the Israelites were attacked by the people of Amalek. Moses told Joshua to go select warriors from the camp to fight and then told him that he, Moses, would stand on top of the nearby hill with the rod of God in his hands. Joshua did what Moses asked, and Moses went up to the top of the hill. As the battle raged, whenever Moses lifted the rod up in the air, the Israelites would win. Whenever he let his hands down, the army of Amalek would begin to prevail. Noticing that Moses's arms were tired from lifting the rod, two men, Aaron and Hur, put a stone down for Moses to sit on, and then the men stood by his side and lifted Moses's arms up—one on one side and one on the other. With the help of these two men, Moses was able to keep his arms raised through the end of the day and the end of the battle.

In this particular battle, it seems like the Lord wanted only Moses to lift the rod. He didn't hand it off to Aaron or Hur to take their turns, but rather they held his arms with the rod the whole time. Aaron and Hur could not take over for Moses—holding the rod was a job uniquely his—but they could sustain him and give him strength to do what God asked him to do. Each man was in his own place carrying out the work of God in his unique and called way.

I often wonder in what ways I can help hold up the arms and the work that the Lord's leaders have been called to do. Their responsibilities may be specific to them, but the work overall is the same. Whether I am called to hold up the rod or hold up the arms, in the end, it is the Lord who prevails in the battle. —DB

Reflect and Respond
How can you hold up the arms of others who have been called to lead?

Your favorite
scripture in
Exodus 17

EXODUS 18:23

**If thou shalt do this thing, and God command thee so,
then thou shalt be able to endure.**

When Moses first left Egypt as a fugitive, he went and lived among the people of Midian. There he met his wife Zipporah and his new father-in-law, Jethro. When he went back into Egypt to deliver the Israelites, his father-in-law did not go, but they met up again while they were journeying out in the wilderness after the exodus. Moses told Jethro all the miracles they had experienced, and "Jethro rejoiced for all the goodness which the Lord had done" (Exodus 18:9).

The next morning, Moses went about his regular duties of hearing the issues of all the people and trying to help them make the proper decisions according to the laws and will of God. Jethro watched as Moses judged the people from the morning until the setting of the sun. When the day was over, Jethro came to Moses with some advice and counsel. He knew that Moses's intention was to help the people to connect with their God, but the way he was doing it would eventually wear him out. "This thing is too heavy for thee" (Exodus 18:18). Jethro's advice was to select God-fearing and faithful leaders among the Israelites to be rulers over thousands, hundreds, fifties, and tens. They would counsel and judge over the smaller matters, and Moses would be able to do the same with the larger ones. Jethro's advice also came with the acknowledgment that this would only be a good idea if "God command thee so" (Exodus 18:23). It was just an idea, and perhaps an inspired one, but Moses should confirm with the Lord.

Moses was doing God's work, just as many of us are called to do, but perhaps there was a better way to do it. He learned that better way from his father-in-law, showing us the beauty of counseling and the brilliant truth that revelation is scattered among us. —DB

Reflect and Respond

When have advice and counsel come into your life that turned out to be inspired?

Your favorite scripture in
Exodus 18

EXODUS 20:2

**I am the Lord thy God, which have brought
thee out of the land of Egypt.**

When the children of Israel came to the foot of Mount Sinai, the Lord informed them that He intended to help them become a kingdom of priests and priestesses—a holy and peculiar people (see Exodus 19). Part of that process would come about because of the covenant relationship they would enter into with God. He would be their God, and they would be His people. And He would show them how to live in this royal way. He would teach them how to be a peculiar people to the Lord. Some of the most well-known instructions on living a holy covenant life are the Ten Commandments, found in Exodus 20. A covenant people would be loyal to their God and not bow down to others. They would remember His holy Sabbath day as a sign of whose they were. They would honor father and mother and promise not to kill, commit adultery, or steal. As His people, His covenant people, they promised to live after this particular code of conduct.

The Ten Commandments could easily be seen as a list of restrictions—a mandate from the Lord to live in a certain way, or else. But in the context of the Lord's promised intention from the chapter before, they are seen as a path to becoming. It's simply the way that holy people live. I have always been moved by the statement that the Lord makes before He introduces the Ten Commandments. Before He gives any instruction, He first reminds the people that He was the one who delivered them from Egypt, that He was a God who heard their cries and sent a deliverer. He was for them—on their side. He had their best interests in mind. Before He taught them, He first reminded them that He loved them. —DB

Reflect and Respond

*What do you know about the Lord that makes you believe He is
good and trustworthy?*

Your favorite
scripture in
Exodus 20

EXODUS 23:20

. . . to keep thee in the way . . .

One afternoon, as twilight began to fall, we left our home and gathered with the Saints in the Conference Center so we could listen to an Apostle of the Lord. He asked us not to lie, cheat, steal, or act immorally. He reminded us to pray, to take care of our bodies, to follow the promptings of the Holy Ghost. He counseled us not to fill our minds with unholy things. He told us true happiness requires us to pay the price of obedience. He suggested that listening to the Holy Ghost should be the quest of a lifetime. As we learn how to do that, we can live in enemy territory and not be deceived or destroyed.

In the time of Moses, the people also gathered together so they could listen to a prophet of the Lord. He asked them not to follow a multitude to do evil (see Exodus 23:2). He reminded them to keep far from false matters, to rest on the Sabbath, to care for the widows and the fatherless (see Exodus 23:7, 12; 22:22). And the people said, "All that the Lord hath said will we do, and be obedient" (Exodus 24:7). Through Moses, the Lord gave counsel with a promise: "Behold, I send an Angel before thee, to keep thee in the way, and to bring thee into the place which I have prepared" (Exodus 23:20). He gave them a way to obtain safety and priceless blessings from the Lord.

It is the same today as it was in times of old. The Lord speaks through His prophets—sending counsel, requiring obedience, extending promises. In this there is safety. In this there is peace. —EBF

Reflect and Respond

What counsel from the prophet or apostles has kept you in the Lord's way?

Your favorite scripture in **Exodus 23**

EXODUS 25:8

That I may dwell among them . . .

As I read about the building up of the tabernacle, my thoughts are filled with beauty. Blue, and purple, and scarlet, and fine linen. Chains of pure gold and beaten work. Silver and brass and precious stones. "Speak unto the children of Israel, that they bring me an offering: of every man that giveth it willingly with his heart ye shall take my offering. . . . And let them make me a sanctuary; that I may dwell among them" (Exodus 25:2, 8).

I am reminded that they are in the wilderness, and I ask myself, *Can such beauty be found in wilderness places?* This offering will require sacrifice. Giving up. Giving all. It will require them to bring their finest to the Lord. Through this bringing of their finest, there is a process of sanctification taking place. A process of consecration.

I study *sanctification* in the dictionary: To make religious. To free from sin. To set apart. I see that it comes from Latin *sanctus,* which means "holy." I begin to understand that sanctification includes letting go. Next I study *consecration:* To make sacred. To devote something exclusively to a particular purpose. To dedicate. I see that it comes from Latin *consecrat,* which means "dedicated" or "devoted," and from Latin *sacer,* which means "sacred." Dedicated sacred. I begin to understand that consecration includes giving everything.

This bringing of their finest would require devotion. The process would become an experience that was sacred to them, one that would make them consecrated. Dedicated. Sacred. Holy. It was necessary, for when Israel is sanctified, they receive the Lord's promise: "And there I will meet with thee, and I will commune with thee" (Exodus 25:22). —EBF

Reflect and Respond

What is your definition of sanctification? *What is your definition of* consecration?

Your favorite scripture in Exodus 25

EXODUS 29:1

**And this is the thing that thou shalt do unto them
to hallow them, to minister unto me.**

The Lord commanded the children of Israel to construct a sacred tabernacle. Within its walls, God would teach them holy patterns, and they would participate in consecrating rituals. Selected from among the people would be some who would serve as priests in the temple to help facilitate the work that would happen there, in some instances representing the Lord Himself. In order to set these people apart for their holy responsibilities, the Lord gave them instructions for certain clothing and ordinances that they would participate in. As He said, these would be the things that they should do "to hallow them, to minister unto me" (Exodus 29:1). To *hallow* means to consecrate or set apart for a holy purpose.

Aaron and his sons would be brought "unto the door of the tabernacle of the congregation" (Exodus 29:4), and they would be washed with water and then have the "anointing oil" (Exodus 29:7) poured upon their heads. Water could represent a cleansing. Holy anointing oil was used at times to signify a person being endowed with the wisdom of heaven. They would also be dressed in clothing that would be fitting for priests in a royal setting. These symbolic acts would remind them of their duties and responsibilities to represent the Lord and participate in His holy work. They were to be set apart for a royal cause and would need to be clean and specifically endowed with certain gifts and privileges in order to do the great work God had for them. —DB

Reflect and Respond

What is the holy purpose God has set you apart for?

Your favorite
scripture in
Exodus 29

EXODUS 32:8

They have turned aside quickly out of the way.

Do you find yourself asking how Israel could have turned from God so quickly? How were they so quick to forget the bondage, the plagues, the parting of the Red Sea? The cloud and the pillar of light? How about the manna? Because it seems like the manna would have kept appearing every morning of the forty mornings Moses was upon the mount. Did they become too commonplace, these miracles in the midst of the ordinary?

"Go, get thee down; for thy people, which thou broughtest out of the land of Egypt, have corrupted themselves: They have turned aside quickly out of the way which I commanded them" (Exodus 32:7–8). I can't help but focus on one phrase, "they have turned aside quickly out of the way," and I am discouraged by Israel's choice. Then I take a good hard look at my own life. Moving from where I am to where I need to be is often harder than I thought. I make the choice for the better, I feel the confirmation as I press forward, but staying the course becomes exhausting. Where I was before seems familiar and more comfortable. And so, I turn aside. Just for a little break. It can happen so quickly.

I can understand Israel's fear that their prophet has disappeared and isn't going to come back. I can hear Moses begging the Lord to give Israel one more chance. And then the Lord answers: "I will do this thing also that thou hast spoken: for thou hast found grace in my sight, and I know thee by name" (Exodus 33:17). The Lord knows each of us by name. He is quick to forgive and extend His love so that we can move forward with Him by our side. —EBF

Reflect and Respond
What keeps you from turning aside quickly out of the way?

Your favorite scripture in Exodus 32

EXODUS 33:14

**My presence shall go with thee,
and I will give thee rest.**

While Moses was receiving more goodness from God on top of Mount Sinai, the people were down at the base of it making a golden calf and worshipping and dancing around it in rebellion.

The Lord sent Moses down the mountain with two stone tablets that were written on by the finger of the Lord—tablets that included more of His covenant instruction. When Moses came down and saw what was happening, he threw down and broke the tablets, almost as if to say the people were not ready for what the Lord had given. After a rebuke from Moses, the people repented and looked to God for mercy. And mercy is what they found.

The Lord's next instructions were to take the people to the promised land, just as He had always intended. He also promised an angel to lead them and His own presence among them. Despite their sin and rebellion, the Lord did not abandon His people. He gave them additional instructions and counsel that would help them to become the holy people He hoped they would be. We refer to these additional instructions as the law of Moses. They were kind of like training wheels that would assist the children of Israel in learning the ways of holiness. The Israelites were taken out of Egypt in a single day, but it would take years to get Egypt out of them. These new instructions and promise of His presence were one more evidence of a God who meets people where they are in order to elevate them further. —DB

Reflect and Respond

When have you found a God of mercy in times of your own temporary rebellion?

Your favorite scripture in Exodus 33

EXODUS 35:21

And they came, **every one whose heart stirred him up . . .**

The first time I read the description "wise hearted" I was immediately intrigued (Exodus 35:10, 25). I wanted to know more about that. I prayed that the Lord would teach my heart that principle. Later that week, I had the opportunity to discuss sacred topics with a group of women. We spoke of hope, trust, faith, optimism, and prosperity. As the topic turned to prosperity, one of the women asked, "What is prosperity? What does it mean in your life?" I said the first thing that came to mind, "Prosperity is when you go to the grocery store and you don't have to spend time looking at the price of every brand of butter to find the cheapest one." That might have been a trivial description, but each of us could relate to having financial burdens. We spoke of all the things we would focus on if money, and professions, and expenses didn't have to occupy so much of our minds.

The next morning, I felt like having warm bread and butter for breakfast. I pulled out the bread and then opened the fridge, only to realize I was completely out of butter. I couldn't help but be reminded of our conversation the night before. I put butter on my grocery shopping list.

Within the hour someone knocked on my front door. It was one of the women I had been with the night before. She stood there on my porch with a pound of butter tied up in white tulle. "I just felt prompted to bring this over this morning," she said simply, "and to say the Lord wants you to have prosperity."

I was momentarily speechless. And then I said, "How did you know I needed butter?" Which was as ridiculously trivial as the definition of prosperity I had given the night before.

"I didn't know," she said. "I just woke up at 4:00 this morning and felt a prompting that you needed butter. This morning. Before I did anything else with my day."

The funny thing is, I could have totally made it through the day without the butter. I would have picked some up that afternoon. I tried to figure out the urgency of the

4:00 a.m. prompting, and then I realized, it wasn't about the butter. It was about the lesson. Because just after the butter came, I read this description of the wise-hearted people found in Exodus, "And they came, every one whose heart stirred him up, and every one whom his spirit made willing, and they brought the Lord's offering to the work" (Exodus 35:21). I followed the footnote for the word *offering,* and it said, "generosity." "And they brought the Lord's generosity."

"And they came, both men and women, as many as were willing hearted" (Exodus 35:22).

"Them hath he filled with wisdom of heart" (Exodus 35:35). "Every wise hearted man, in whose heart the Lord had put wisdom, even every one whose heart stirred him up to come unto the work to do it" (Exodus 36:2).

I thought about my friend. The one whose heart had been stirred up. The one whose spirit was willing. The one who brought the Lord's generosity. The one whom the Lord had filled with wisdom of heart. She who had a willing heart, who didn't think it might be odd to drop off a pound of butter to someone who was perfectly capable of obtaining her own, but took the wisdom of the Lord in her heart and then acted. Through her willing and wise heart, I learned an extremely powerful lesson. Because of a pound of butter. —EBF

Reflect and Respond

How might you be the means of extending the Lord's generosity to someone, somehow, today?

Your favorite scripture in Exodus 35

EXODUS 36:7

**For the stuff they had was sufficient for
all the work . . . , and too much.**

My friend has an old milk barn. He recently started working on fixing it up. He has great plans for it. It's going to take a lot of work, and he spends a lot of time there. One day, when it's finished, it will be a blessing to his family because of his sacrifice. Because of his time. Because of his vision of what it could be. It will become a place of refuge.

The story of the people of Israel building the tabernacle matches this pattern. The Lord gave Moses a vision of what his people could become, but it was going to take a lot of work and a lot of time. First, Moses taught his people what it meant to be obedient. He spoke of repentance, and they became sanctified. He asked them to give, to keep back nothing. And the people brought "*much more than enough* for the service of the work" (Exodus 36:5; emphasis added). Within the giving, his people learned what it meant to become consecrated. Then, on the very last day, after all the elements were ready, one final thing took place. "And they made the plate of the holy crown of pure gold, and wrote upon it a writing, like to the engravings of a signet, HOLINESS TO THE LORD. . . . Thus was all the work of the tabernacle of the tent of the congregation finished" (Exodus 39:30–32). It wasn't until "Holiness to the Lord" had been fastened upon the mitre that the work was finished. And for Israel it became a place of refuge.

I wonder to myself, *where am I in this process?* Sometimes my life looks like the old milk barn, and I hope Someone has some great plans for it, a vision, even if I can't see it right now. I am willing to work hard, to give sufficient and too much. To bring my finest. When I am finished, I want my life to be holiness to the Lord. I want to find in Him my refuge. —EBF

Reflect and Respond
Where is your place of refuge in the Lord?

Your favorite scripture in Exodus 36

EXODUS 39:30

And they made the plate of the holy crown of pure gold, and wrote upon it . . . HOLINESS TO THE LORD.

The descriptions of the elements of the tabernacle and the clothing of the priests who would serve in it are nothing short of exquisite. The finery is especially impressive considering the Israelites were a traveling group of people wandering in the wilderness. The colors and materials would make you feel like you were visiting a palace. There was blue, purple, and scarlet linen. There were materials coated with the finest gold. There were precious gems and curious workmanship. Truly it was to be the house of a King.

One of my favorite elements in the tabernacle was on the robes of the high priest. Along the hem were pomegranates made of red, blue, and purple linen. And in between each pomegranate was a bell of pure gold. I like to imagine the sound of the ringing bell as the high priest moved about the temple. Even those who were outside its curtained walls might still be able to hear the jingling of the bells. Perhaps it would make them think of the holy work that was being done inside, a constant reminder of God among them.

I also like to think about the pomegranates with their countless seeds, a possible reminder to them of the promises made to Abraham, Isaac, and Jacob of posterity and blessings innumerable as the stars of heaven.

Each element of the tabernacle and clothing was symbolic, designed to point the children of Israel to something holy. Even the plaque across the forehead of the high priest bore the words HOLINESS TO THE LORD—a reminder of the purpose behind everything that was happening inside the temple walls and hopefully inside the walls of the people's hearts. —DB

Reflect and Respond

What reminders do you have in your home that make you think of God and His holiness?

Your favorite scripture in Exodus 39

EXODUS 40:16

**Thus did Moses: according to all that the
Lord commanded him, so did he.**

The first day of the first month was going to be exciting. The Lord had initially given the instructions on how to build the tabernacle to Moses on Mount Sinai. The people had been busy at work. They had donated their time, skills, materials, and wisdom to the building of each piece. They also donated their precious stones and items for the adorning of everything in it. Then the commandment came to rear the tabernacle. I like to imagine a buzz throughout the camp of Israel that day as people worked to lift the walls and strike the stakes into the ground.

The Lord was very specific about the order of where and when things would be placed inside. First, the holy ark of the testimony, followed by the tables with the candlesticks and the lighting of the lamps. Then the altar of gold for the burning of incense within the holy place, and the altar for burnt sacrifices without. Each item had its place and purpose, and everything was set up in order until the last of the details were done.

As you read through the instructions, you can't help but notice a line repeated several times. "Thus did Moses: according to all that the Lord commanded him, so did he" (Exodus 40:16; see also vv. 19, 21, 23, 25). Don't you want that said about you? She or he does "according to all that the Lord commanded." And when it was all done by Moses, just as the Lord commanded, a cloud of His presence rested upon the temple, and His glory filled the tabernacle. In that precious place, God would teach a pattern of living—a template for a holy life. As the children of Israel lived according to all He would command, His spirit and glory would rest upon them as well. —DB

Reflect and Respond

When have you experienced the spirit and glory of God resting upon you?

Your favorite
scripture in
Exodus 40

LEVITICUS 6:13

The fire shall ever be burning.

The book of Leviticus can feel overwhelming. Here are three hints I have found helpful when reading this particular book in the Old Testament.

Watch for Symbolism

Leviticus 6 talks about the fire upon the altar: "It shall not be put out . . . the fire shall ever be burning upon the altar; it shall never go out" (Leviticus 6:12–13). Consider the symbolism of the Savior and His Atonement that is captured within that verse, the idea of a fire ever burning that shall never go out. Beautiful.

Understand Sacrifice

It is helpful to study *sacrifice* in the Bible Dictionary before you study Leviticus. It makes the symbolism in the first half of Leviticus so much easier to understand. For example, the presentation of the sacrifice was made by the sacrificer himself. It was personal. Individual. There is great importance in that. The next step was the laying on of hands to dedicate the animal to God as a substitute for the sacrificer. The sprinkling of blood became symbolic of Christ's blood that would be shed. Burning the sacrifice symbolized the consecration of the worshipper to Jehovah. The word *sacrifice* comes from *sacer*, which means "sacred," and *fice*, which means "to make." *To make sacred.*

Learn about Consecration

According to Bible scholar Alfred Edersheim, the subject matter for the book of Leviticus is consecration on the part of Israel. The first half explains the manner of access to God, and the second part explains the holiness which is the result of that access.[10]

The book of Leviticus explains how to gain access to God through:

- sacrifice—Leviticus 1–7
- priesthood—Leviticus 8–10
- worship—Leviticus 11–14

- family life—Leviticus 12
- participation in a congregation—Leviticus 13–15
- the Day of Atonement—Leviticus 16

It also describes the holiness that characterizes the people of God:

- personal holiness—Leviticus 17
- holiness in the family—Leviticus 18
- holiness in social relations—Leviticus 19–20
- holiness in the priesthood—Leviticus 21–22
- holy seasons—Leviticus 23–24
- holiness of the land—Leviticus 25
- the blessing attached to faithful observance of the covenant—Leviticus 26
- the freewill offerings of the heart—Leviticus 27

—EBF

Reflect and Respond

What are you looking forward to most in your study of Leviticus?

Your favorite scripture in Leviticus 6

LEVITICUS 18:4

… keep mine ordinances, **to walk therein** …

Sometimes the path is clearly marked. Black and white. This is true here in the book of Leviticus. The caution that makes up chapter 18 is the stuff that makes up our day. It fills the sitcoms and movies and novels. We see it on the news. We find it on the internet. Everything the Lord has cautioned against can permeate the walls of our own homes.

The Lord doesn't just outline the dangers in this chapter, He also describes the path we should walk: "I am the Lord your God. After the doings of the land of Egypt, wherein ye dwelt, shall ye not do: and after the doings of the land of Canaan, whither I bring you, shall ye not do: *neither shall ye walk* in their ordinances" (Leviticus 18:2–3; emphasis added). On the one hand, do not be Egypt. Let go of your past sins. Do not walk the path they trod. On the other hand, do not be Canaan. There will be days of temptation ahead of you. Do not follow their footsteps. It is clear—these are the two paths we should not walk. Instead: "Ye shall do my judgments, and keep mine ordinances, *to walk therein:* I am the Lord your God. . . . Keep my statutes, . . . which if a man do, he shall live in them: I am the Lord" (Leviticus 18:4–5; emphasis added).

It is hard work, this staying on the clear path—to walk out of the movie unfinished, to set down the novel unread, to turn off a favorite sitcom without rationalizing that one part. Sometimes we might feel alone on this path. But we must remember the promise of the Lord, "If ye will obey my voice indeed, and keep my covenant, then ye shall be *a peculiar treasure* unto me . . . and ye shall be unto me . . . an holy nation" (Exodus 19:5–6; emphasis added). Don't be Egypt, don't be Canaan, He cautions. Choose to be a holy nation. *Be Israel.* —EBF

Reflect and Respond

How can you walk on His path today?

Your favorite scripture in Leviticus 18

LEVITICUS 22:32

I am the Lord which hallow you.

"Speak . . . unto all the children of Israel, and say unto them, Whatsoever he be of the house of Israel . . . that will offer his oblation . . . unto the Lord . . . ye shall offer at your own will" (Leviticus 22:18–19). I wonder what Israel felt in this moment of the journey. This learning how to sacrifice requires trust. The sacrifice was more than just a male animal without blemish, it was the giving of their heart. Had they experienced enough of the aching, the tearstains, the time on their knees, the spirit worn down, the regret, the being broken to understand?

Were they finally humble enough to trust the Lord, who had brought them out of Egypt? Because now the offering He asks of Israel is that they become holy, live righteously, love their neighbor, and keep the commandments. My heart recognizes these as offerings of the soul. The whole soul.

Did you notice that after each verse of commandment the same phrase is found at the bottom? A reminder of Who is making the request. The repetition becomes constant. Familiar.

I am the Lord your God. I am the Lord. *Trust me.*

At the end of the chapter the Lord gives the reason behind the keeping of His commandments, " . . . but I will be hallowed among the children of Israel: I am the Lord which hallow you, that brought you out of the land of Egypt, to be your God: I am the Lord" (Leviticus 22:32–33).

Your offering is an oblation made of your own will with your whole soul. A sacrifice that would hallow you. An offering that would make you wholly holy. —EBF

Reflect and Respond

Why would keeping the commandments make you holy?

Your favorite
scripture in
Leviticus 22

LEVITICUS 23:32

It shall be unto you a sabbath of rest.

When I was in Jerusalem, I fell in love with the Sabbath. Someone had told me before I went that I needed to go to the Western Wall of the ancient temple to welcome in the Sabbath with the faithful gatherers. "Do not miss it," they pleaded. Because the Jewish Sabbath begins at sundown on Friday night, people scampered to prepare their homes and lives for the upcoming day. All day long people greeted and parted with the phrase *Shabbat Shalom,* which means peaceful Sabbath. The streets bustled as the sun was setting. It felt like Christmas Eve. There was contagious anticipation in the air. As I approached the wall, Jews dressed in traditional clothing scurried to the remaining ruins, often with children following quickly in their shadows. The excitement was brewing. I was giddy about an unknown gift that I knew was going to be good.

For over four hundred years the Israelites were in bondage to the Egyptians. For four centuries they were slaves: tired, beaten, tear-filled. And then it was over. When Israel left Egypt, the Lord introduced days of feasts and Sabbaths as a way to honor Him and to remember their deliverance. The people learned to celebrate their Sabbaths, because now they could.

This feeling has not left the land of Jerusalem. As the sun set that beautiful Sabbath eve, I closed my eyes and listened. I heard voices reciting scripture. Voices in song. Voices in prayer. Some pleaded for help and others poured out their heart in thanksgiving. Soon people began to form circles and sing and dance as they welcomed the Sabbath in like an honored guest. I stood in the middle of it all and soaked it in. For the people in Jerusalem the Sabbath is a day of jubilee. There is reason to celebrate. —DB

....

Reflect and Respond
How do you celebrate the Sabbath?

Your favorite scripture in **Leviticus 23**

NUMBERS 6:24

The Lord **bless thee, and keep thee.**

As I started to read the book of Numbers, I tried to keep track of all of the numbers in my head—the men, the tribes, the tents. They even numbered the sacrifices—by weight, by quantity, by the bowls they were brought in. *But why keep a record of so many numbers?* With this careful counting of men and tribes, was the Lord trying to teach us a lesson? I am reminded of a verse from the book of Moses: "All things are numbered unto me, for they are mine and I know them" (Moses 1:35). Was the Lord trying to help us understand the worth of a soul? Before they started this great journey into the wilderness, a census was taken, and every person was accounted for. Numbered. Was the hope that not one would be lost?

The Hebrew Bible shows the name of this book as *Journey through the Wilderness.* After crossing the Red Sea, after spending two years receiving the laws and commandments and preparing, the children of Israel began their Journey through the Wilderness.

My favorite part is that this journey began with numbering and then included a blessing from the Lord—one that was personal and individualized, a promise to covenant Israel, not as a whole but individually. "On this wise ye shall bless the children of Israel, saying unto them, The Lord bless thee, and keep thee: The Lord make his face shine upon thee, and be gracious unto thee: The Lord lift up his countenance upon thee, and give thee peace. And they shall put my name upon the children of Israel; and I will bless them" (Numbers 6:23–27).

Wherever you are on your journey, whatever your wilderness place may be, remember you are numbered of the Lord. He will bless thee and keep thee. Watch for Him there. —EBF

Reflect and Respond
Have you felt numbered by the Lord? How has He blessed you and kept you?

Your favorite scripture in **Numbers 6**

NUMBERS 9:23

At the commandment of the Lord they rested... and at
the commandment of the Lord they journeyed.

Just so you know, I am awful with directions. I get lost on streets in my own home-town. It stresses me out to not know where I am going, and it happens all the time. One of the things I appreciate most about the map app on my phone is the style it gives directions in. Before I begin, I can see the entire route. Then as I go, it not only gives step-by-step turns, but it also keeps me updated along the way: "In two miles you will be turning right." I appreciate that kind of heads-up.

This is a style of directions the children of Israel may have appreciated as well. They were in an unknown wilderness. They didn't know where or how far away the promised land was. They had no idea when they would get there. They didn't get a step-by-step plan for the journey. Instead, they literally followed the Lord each new day. When they would stop, a cloud would rest on the tabernacle by day and a pillar of fire at night. When it was time to go, the cloud would move, and the children of Israel would follow. When the cloud rested again, they would stop and set up camp. Sometimes they were in a place for two days, sometimes a month or even a year. They didn't know when they would move until the cloud moved.

At times it may have been frustrating not knowing when they would rest or when they would journey. Perhaps a plan or schedule would have been comforting or nice. But the Lord was not teaching them how to be comfortable. He was teaching them how to follow Him, and how to trust Him new each day. —DB

Reflect and Respond

When have you followed the Lord day by day not knowing the details, but learning to trust?

Your favorite
scripture in
Numbers 9

NUMBERS 11:20

Why came we forth out of Egypt?

I have never had the same food over and over again for days on end, so I don't know how the Israelites felt eating their manna every single day. But after a long amount of time collecting and eating it, the children of Israel began to complain to Moses about the bread that fell from heaven. "What about the cucumbers we had in Egypt," they said to each other. "And the melons and the onion and the garlic!" "But now our soul is dried away: there is nothing at all, beside this manna, before our eyes" (Numbers 11:5–6). The journey was certainly hard, and the conditions out in the wilderness must not have been easy. It is not surprising they complained and then wondered whether they should have even left Egypt in the first place. But perhaps they forgot what life in Egypt was like. They were slaves! From sunup to sundown they worked under the burdens of Pharaoh. Life was *not* better back in Egypt. It was good for them to leave and be led by God to their land of promise. And along the way, they did and would continue to see His miracles—often in the ordinary moments of their day.

Sometimes moving forward is difficult. The journey can be unknown and the conditions uncomfortable. But that discomfort might be the sign you are moving in the right direction. Progression has always been stretching to the soul. The road may be rough, but it is headed to promises fulfilled. There will be evidence of God with you daily along the way, and it is good to remember and count where you see His hand. Sometimes it comes in such simple ways we might overlook it. Try not to let the monotony of the mundane blind you from the miracles. —DB

Reflect and Respond

As you look back on yesterday, are you able to see the miraculous in the mundane?

Your favorite scripture in Numbers 11

NUMBERS 12:15

The people journeyed not till Miriam was brought in again.

I once heard a new bishop tell his congregation that the people who were most surprised by his call and ordination were himself and his own family. The role of a bishop is no more important than any other in a ward, but perhaps the reason the family members were surprised is because they had an expectation of how a bishop should be and act. They were familiar with his weaknesses. They could see his humanity up close and personal. For some, it is hard to balance the humanity and mistakes of a person with their ability to lead and give counsel and direction in a divine way. Many people have this similar struggle with prophets and apostles. They know they are prone to mistakes, but they also believe they are inspired. So, when are they wrong? Or are they? What mistakes would God allow? If any? And is it our job to question?

It is hard to know what actually happened between Moses and his siblings during this certain day of their journey. But we read that Miriam, his sister, spoke against Moses. Her language makes it seem like she was making her own judgment and accusing him of stepping beyond his bounds as the prophet. Perhaps he had done something wrong, and maybe she could have done it better. Moses's response was humility, but the Lord had a lesson to teach Miriam. We must remember that the Lord does not condemn questions, but it seems that Miriam's questions were some that, if left unchecked, would ruin her. She was struck with leprosy—perhaps an outward manifestation of an inward disease. Although she was clearly in the wrong, Moses pleaded for her healing, and the Lord did not move the camp until it came. Miriam might have had a lesson to learn, but she would not be left behind in the learning of it. —DB

Reflect and Respond

How do you deal with the fallibility of mortal leaders while honoring the inspiration they receive?

Your favorite scripture in Numbers 12

NUMBERS 13:30

Let us go up at once . . . for we are well able to overcome it.

From twelve men who were chosen because of their bravery, their leadership, and their character, two stand out as heroes: Caleb, who had another spirit with him and followed the Lord fully (see Numbers 14:24), and Joshua, whose name was changed from Oshea, meaning *help,* to Jehoshua, meaning *Jehovah is help.* This was the same Joshua whom Moses counseled to be strong and of a good courage (see Deuteronomy 31:6).

The heroic endeavors of these two men were a direct result of their character. Of the twelve men who saw the promised land, ten saw great walls and a strong army. They spoke of giants and compared themselves to grasshoppers. They brought back an evil report. Only two brought back a good report. They spoke of a land flowing with milk and honey. They saw the danger but were not hindered, saying, "Let us go up at once . . . for we are well able to overcome it" (Numbers 13:30).

Two of the twelve were filled with optimism. With hope. With faith. Nothing was going to hold them back from what the Lord had asked them to accomplish. They were strong men of a great courage who knew the Lord was with them (see Numbers 14:9). A promise was given to these two heroes because of their devotion, because of their bravery, because they fully followed the Lord. Of the entire generation, only these two were allowed to enter the promised land. "Surely none of the men shall see . . . because they have not wholly followed me: Save Caleb . . . and Joshua . . . for they have wholly followed the Lord" (Numbers 32:11–12). Two heroes: one known for fully following the Lord, one who believed Jehovah is help. —EBF

Reflect and Respond

Why do you feel optimism is often a heroic characteristic?

Your favorite scripture in Numbers 13

NUMBERS 15:39

And it shall be unto you for a fringe,
that ye may look upon it, and remember.

One night my family was invited to gather to a high mountain overlooking the valley below, with friends who had come to remember a sweet girl born on a February day two years before. She was privileged to spend a few hours with her loving family—just long enough to leave a gentle impression on their hearts—and then she returned home to heaven.

In her mother's heart, this dear, sweet baby will always be remembered as a celebration—so we were asked to write down a celebration in our life and tie it to the end of a balloon. For a few quiet moments our thoughts were drawn inward, and then we wrote down our celebrations on pale pink cards and tied them to balloons. We stood there in a circle and sang softly, a melody of words to remind us that families can be forever. The testimony of that truth burned in my heart and streamed in wet tears down my cheeks. Then the baby's mother asked us to let go of our balloons in celebration. And we remembered, and our eyes lifted heavenward.

Today Moses teaches a lesson on the importance of remembering. "Speak unto the children of Israel, and bid them that they make them fringes in the borders of their garments . . . that they put upon the fringe of the borders a ribband of blue: And it shall be unto you for a fringe, that ye may look upon it, and remember all the commandments of the Lord, and do them . . . and be holy" (Numbers 15:38–40).

I love this thought of fringes, and it makes me wonder, do we have fringes today, like the pink balloons that led our hearts to remember? Do we have fringes that we can look upon to remind us of the commandments of the Lord, to draw our eyes heavenward? —EBF

Reflect and Respond

What are the fringes you look upon to remind you of the commandments of the Lord?

Your favorite scripture in
Numbers 15

NUMBERS 20:4

**Why have ye brought up the congregation of
the Lord into this wilderness . . . ?**

When the camp of Israel arrived at the place named Kadesh, in the desert of Zin, they discovered that there was no water. The people's reaction makes it seem like the situation was pretty desperate. They thought they were going to die. In their anxiety and anger, they asked Moses and Aaron, "Why have you brought us into this wilderness? Why did you lead us to a place where we will just die?" (see Numbers 20:4). As was typical for them, Moses and Aaron went and bowed themselves down before the Lord to plead for help and answers. The answer was for the two brother leaders to gather the whole camp of Israel to a rock that was in front of the camp.

In what seems like a moment of frustration, Moses called the camp together in front of the rock and then said, "Hear now, ye rebels; must we fetch you water out of this rock?" (Numbers 20:10). Then Moses took his staff and hit the rock twice, and water came gushing out.

Water is not supposed to gush out of rocks—the same way seas are not supposed to open. When the Israelites complained against Moses, they asked him why *he* had brought them into the wilderness. But it wasn't Moses. It was the Lord. And when Moses chided the Israelites and asked, "must *we* fetch you water," it wasn't Moses and Aaron who would get the water. Again, it was the Lord. The Lord who does the impossible. The Lord who makes the way open. The Lord who can make rocks gush water in a barren desert wilderness and dry ground appear from the floor of a sea. It was important for them, and perhaps important for us on our own journeys, to remember who is actually leading the camp. —DB

Reflect and Respond

*When have you seen God do something that isn't typically what is
"supposed" to happen?*

Your favorite
scripture in
Numbers 20

NUMBERS 21:4

And the soul of the people was much discouraged because of the way.

Have you ever read the scripture in First Nephi that talks about the people who were bit by the fiery flying serpents and wondered what that was all about? For years I was intrigued by the phrase, "and the labor which they had to perform was to look; and because of the simpleness of the way, or the easiness of it, there were many who perished" (1 Nephi 17:41). Why did they perish? One of the gifts of reading the Old Testament is that it can strengthen our understanding of what we have read previously in the other standard works. This is true here; Numbers 21 can help us better understand what we read in 1 Nephi 17.

In Numbers we are taught about the people who were "much discouraged because of the way" (Numbers 21:4). I know what it is to be discouraged because of the way, to lose sight of the goal, focusing instead on what is getting me down. In the midst of this discouragement, the people began to murmur. It wasn't new murmuring; it was the same complaints they stumbled on every time: Why did we leave Egypt? To die in the wilderness? Because of the murmuring, the Lord sent fiery flying serpents among the people. Those who were bit, died. As they became humbled from this plague, they begged Moses to ask the Lord to take away the serpents. The Lord's answer for healing was easy—just look to the staff Moses held, and they would be healed and live. In essence, look to Christ. But Nephi tells us they didn't—because it was too simple. Too easy. Instead, they perished.

Maybe your soul is discouraged because of the way. Maybe you are desperate for healing. The answer is easy: Look to Christ, dear friend, and live. —EBF

Reflect and Respond
How can you look to God?

Your favorite scripture in
Numbers 21

NUMBERS 22:34

I have sinned; **for I knew not** that
thou stoodest in the way.

In case we missed the lesson on looking to God the first time it was given, with the staff Moses held, the book of Numbers teaches it again, this time through the story of Balaam.

Balak offered Balaam money and cattle and great honor if he would curse Israel. But the Lord made it clear that was not what He wanted Balaam to do: "Thou shalt not curse the people: for they are blessed" (Numbers 22:12). Balaam knew he shouldn't go with the princes of Moab, and yet he rose in the morning, saddled his ass, and went. The Lord wasn't happy with his choice, so He sent an angel to stand in the way so that he wouldn't be able to proceed.

But Balaam didn't look.

The ass, however, saw the angel and would not move. After much struggle between the ass and the rock and the hard place and the narrow way, the Lord finally opened the eyes of Balaam, and he saw the angel standing there. His response is important, "I have sinned; for I knew not that thou stoodest in the way" (Numbers 22:34). *I knew not.*

What prevented him from seeing?

Again, we are reminded of the counsel from Nephi and the lesson that comes from the flying serpents in Numbers 21, "And the labor which they had to perform was to look" (1 Nephi 17:41).

Perhaps we need to become better at looking: for healing. For direction. For counsel. For answers. For miracles. For daily mercies. For angels. For whatever it is the Lord wants us to see.

Today. —EBF

Reflect and Respond

What does the story of Balaam teach you to do when you are between a rock and a hard place?

Your favorite
scripture in
Numbers 22

NUMBERS 27:12

Get thee up into this mount **. . . and see the land.**

I have become attached to Moses. The book of Numbers has given me a great love and admiration for a man I knew very little about before I read the entire Old Testament. Saying farewell is tugging at my heartstrings. This part of the story is hard to take in. It is hard to fathom why Moses isn't the prophet who leads Israel into the promised land. Our hearts wonder if it is fair. We might argue that he *earned* the right. But from Moses we learn an important lesson—God's will for us is good. Always. We must trust that principle even when we don't understand it. Often, the perfect end we conceive in our hearts falls short of the great things the Lord has in store for us.

From Moses we learn that sometimes the Lord prepares a different ending from what we had envisioned, but it is always the right ending. "And the Lord said unto Moses, Get thee up into this mount . . . and see the land which I have given unto the children of Israel. And when thou hast seen it, thou also shalt be gathered unto thy people. . . . And Moses spake unto the Lord, saying, Let the Lord . . . set a man over the congregation, which may go out before them . . . and which may bring them in. . . . And the Lord said unto Moses, take thee Joshua . . . and give him a charge in their sight" (Numbers 27:12–19).

It is touching to see how meekly Moses received the sentence from the Lord. Faithful to the end over his people, his chief concern was that God would appoint a new leader to guide the children of Israel. Once he knew the people would be cared for, his thoughts shifted to the pain of not being with them as they entered the promised land. In Moses's weakness we see so clearly a hint of our own. Moses longed to share what was before Israel. Of course he wanted to have part in the conquest and the rest that would follow in the promised land. "He had believed in it; he had preached it; he had prayed for it; he had laboured, borne, fought for it. And now within reach and view of it *must* he lay himself down to die?"[11]

Scripture records, with touching detail, what passed between Moses and the Lord. "O

Lord God, *thou hast begun* to shew thy servant thy greatness, and thy mighty hand. . . . I pray thee, let me go over, and see the good land that is beyond Jordan. . . . And the Lord said unto me, *Let it suffice thee;* speak no more unto me of this matter" (Deuteronomy 3:24–26; emphasis added). Two phrases within that verse stand out to me: *thou hast begun* and *Let it suffice thee.* First, we learn that Moses had *just begun* to see the greatness of the Lord. In 120 years, at the very end of his life, he had just begun. There is a great lesson there. And second, I love the words *let it suffice thee*—as if the Lord was saying, *This is enough, find joy in this much, and then trust me.* Moses would not lead the people into the promised land, but he would have the privilege of seeing it, and then he would have to trust the will of the Lord, *that it was good.*

"Thus, amid the respectful silence of a mourning people, Moses set out alone upon his last journey. All the way up to the highest top of Pisgah the eyes of the people must have followed him. They could watch him as he stood there in the sunset, taking his full view of the land—there to see for himself how true and faithful Jehovah had been."[12]

When we think of Moses we must remember, he *did* stand on the goodly mountain *within* the promised land. And we must also remember that there, on the top of Pisgah, God prepared something better for Moses than even entrance into that land. "And there arose not a prophet since in Israel like unto Moses, whom the Lord knew face to face" (Deuteronomy 34:10). —EBF

Reflect and Respond

What promises of God are you holding on to right now? What is giving you hope and trust?

Your favorite scripture in
Numbers 27

DEUTERONOMY 2:3

Ye have compassed this mountain long enough.

The book of Deuteronomy is probably one of my favorite books in the Old Testament. What some might call a repeat of the events we just read about in Numbers is really a book filled with tender memories as Moses looks back over the forty-year journey through the wilderness.

Moses begins by reminding the people how they took their journey into the wilderness by way of the Red Sea and compassed Mount Seir for many days. Finally the Lord said, "Ye have compassed this mountain long enough: turn you northward" (Deuteronomy 2:3). I am intrigued by this thought. In my mind I can almost hear the Lord saying, "You have journeyed through this place long enough. It is time to walk away from it. Leave it behind now. Let it go." The Lord allows time for growing, for stretching, for wandering, for gaining strength. But there will come a day, in the midst of these experiences, when we will hear the quiet whisper from the Lord, "Ye have compassed this mountain long enough." Lesson one: move forward.

The Lord told Moses that walking past this mountain wouldn't necessarily be easy. In fact, others would lie in the path. His counsel was clear: "Meddle not with them" (Deuteronomy 2:5). Sometimes we have to move past what could hold us back in order to reach the promised end. Lesson two: meddle not with them.

The chapter ends with two important messages: "Now rise up, said I, and get you over," and "Rise ye up, take your journey" (Deuteronomy 2:13, 24). Perhaps the only way we can move through the hardest days and on to the promised end is to follow this counsel and rise above them. Lesson three: Rise above.

Maybe my favorite lesson in the whole book of Deuteronomy, though, and perhaps in the entire Old Testament, is in verse 7. Throughout their forty-year journey through the wilderness, the people of Israel did not travel alone. Moses reminds them, "For the Lord thy God . . . knoweth thy walking through this great wilderness: these forty years *the*

Lord thy God hath been with thee; thou hast lacked nothing" (Deuteronomy 2:7; emphasis added).

Think about the mountain moments you have journeyed through, the great wilderness places of your life. Comfort fills my heart when I realize the Lord *knows* about the mountain, and He *knows* about the walking through the wilderness. He knows. He doesn't just watch us from above as we are traveling through that place—He is there with us, beside the mountain, within the wilderness. Looking back at the mountain and wilderness moments of my life with a perspective focused on Him, I realize a powerful truth: as empty and heavy as my heart was, I lacked nothing. The Lord filled the empty places and lifted my heavy heart.

Often the wilderness places of our life provide for some of the greatest miracles. Within the journey we are able to witness moments with the Lord if our eyes are open to see. The Lord knows how to lift. He has the capacity to strengthen us until we can move forward again. Along the way we must remember, the Lord *is* completely aware of our journey through every great wilderness.

Lesson four: He will guide us beyond the mountain. He will be with us every step of the wilderness journey. He will make sure that we lack nothing. —EBF

Reflect and Respond
Which of these four lessons do you need most right now?

Your favorite scripture in
Deuteronomy 2

DEUTERONOMY 4:10

Specially the day . . .

As the people of Israel prepared to enter the promised land, Moses took time to give them great counsel. "Take heed to thyself, and keep thy soul diligently, lest thou forget the things which thine eyes have seen, and lest they depart from thy heart all the days of thy life: but teach them thy sons, and thy sons' sons; *specially the day* that thou stoodest before the Lord thy God in Horeb, when the Lord said unto me, Gather me the people together, . . . and ye came near and stood under the mountain; and the mountain burned with fire unto the midst of heaven (Deuteronomy 4:9–11; emphasis added). Moses knew that the burning-mountain moment had been a life-changing experience for those who recognized what it was. He wanted them always to remember what their eyes had seen, never to forget that moment in their hearts. I love how Moses urged them to remember "*specially the day.*"

Elder Ronald A. Rasband encourages us to "think of the special experiences you have been blessed with in your life that have given you conviction and joy in your heart. Remember when you first knew that Joseph Smith was God's prophet of the Restoration? . . . Remember when you received an answer to fervent prayer and realized that your Heavenly Father knows and loves you personally? As you contemplate such special experiences, don't they give you a sense of gratitude and resolve to go forward with renewed faith and determination? . . . In these days of worldly intrusions into our lives, when trials and difficulties may seem to engulf us, let us remember our own special spiritual experiences."[13] —EBF

Reflect and Respond

What is one of the special days you have experienced recently?

Your favorite
scripture in
Deuteronomy 4

DEUTERONOMY 6:6

And these words . . . **shall be in thine heart.**

In Deuteronomy 6 we read the *Shema Yisrael,* the Jewish prayer that is written and wrapped up and placed in the mezuzah that hangs next to the door of Jewish homes. "And these words, which I command thee this day, shall be in thine heart: And thou shalt teach them diligently unto thy children, and shalt talk of them when thou sittest in thine house, and when thou walkest by the way, and when thou liest down, and when thou risest up. And thou shalt bind them for a sign upon thine hand, and they shall be as frontlets between thine eyes. And thou shalt write them upon the posts of thy house, and on thy gates" (Deuteronomy 6:6–9).

When I read these verses, my thoughts turn to the scriptures. His words. I want to make sure I have made a place for them in my heart, and that I teach them diligently to my children. I want to talk about them when we gather together in our house, and when I walk with friends by the way. I want to read them before I lie down, and again when I rise up. I want them to be constantly before my eyes—upon the walls of my home, written on the posts, and upon the gates. All His words, so they will always be in my heart.

I have spent some time pondering how well I am doing at following this counsel, because I really want to learn how to walk after the Lord. Sometimes it's good to take a moment to reflect on your week. Have you found sweet moments as you read the words of the Lord? Are His words finding a place in your heart? —EBF

Reflect and Respond
What is a favorite scripture verse that you keep in your heart?

Your favorite scripture in **Deuteronomy 6**

DEUTERONOMY 7:7

The Lord did not set his love upon you . . . because ye
were more . . . **for ye were the fewest.**

My husband was a lacrosse coach, and I can attest that tryouts were stressful. He never just chose the boys with the *most* talents. Sometimes he chose the ones with the *fewest*. It was not about the winning for him. He will tell you it was, but it wasn't. It was about the boys. The thing I love most about the coach and his team tryout is this: everyone who tried out for the team made it onto either the A team or the B team. No one was cut. He chose to keep every single boy.

It reminds me a little bit of a lesson in the book of Deuteronomy. "The Lord did not set his love upon you, nor choose you, *because ye were more* in number than any people; *for ye were the fewest* of all people: But because the Lord loved you, . . . [he] brought you out with a mighty hand" (Deuteronomy 7:7–8; emphasis added). "And he will love thee, and bless thee, and multiply thee. . . . Thou shalt be blessed above all people" (Deuteronomy 7:13–14). I love that the Lord didn't choose Israel because they were more—because in reality they were the fewest. He did what He did for them because He loved them. That's why He was faithful to them. And He believed in their potential, enough to bring them out with a mighty hand. I believe He will do the same for us.

Do you ever have one of those days when you look back and wonder if you were enough? If anyone even recognized your effort? Do you ever wonder whose team you are on? If anyone is cheering for you? If someone else has more to offer than you ever could? On those days maybe you could remember these verses. The Lord has chosen you because He thinks you are special. You don't have to be more than anyone else; He knows your potential. He has chosen you. —EBF

Reflect and Respond
Why have you chosen to be on the Lord's team?

Your favorite
scripture in
Deuteronomy 7

DEUTERONOMY 28:2

And all these blessings **shall come on thee, and overtake thee**.

President Russell M. Nelson asked: "What is the Lord willing to do for Israel? The Lord has pledged that He will 'fight [our] battles, and [our] children's battles, and our children's children's [battles] . . . to the third and fourth generation'! As you study your scriptures . . . I encourage you to make a list of all that the Lord has promised He will do for covenant Israel. I think you will be astounded! Ponder these promises. Talk about them with your family and friends. Then live and watch for these promises to be fulfilled in your own life."[14]

The Old Testament is rich with the blessings to covenant Israel. One of my favorites is this: "When thou goest out . . . be not afraid . . . for the Lord thy God is with thee . . . let not your hearts faint, fear not, and do not tremble, neither be ye terrified . . . for the Lord your God is he that goeth with you" (Deuteronomy 20:1–4). As you become a collector of the promises, you will find that this is a major theme: God has promised to be with us.

But there are more promises than just that one. Deuteronomy 28 contains a list of blessings for Israel that starts: "And all these blessings shall come on thee, and overtake thee, if thou shalt hearken unto the voice of the Lord thy God" (Deuteronomy 28:2). I love the thought of blessings that come on us and overtake us. We can feel God's abundance in the city and in the field, in our basket, with our children and our professions, and in our coming in and our going out. "The Lord shall open unto thee his good treasure . . . and to bless all the work of thine hand" (Deuteronomy 28:12). So many blessings can be ours if we allow the Lord to be our God and receive His promises to His family. —EBF

Reflect and Respond

Have you had a blessing come upon you or overtake you? What was it?

Your favorite scripture in **Deuteronomy 28**

JOSHUA 1:9

Be strong and of a good courage.

I love this idea often attributed to Norman Vincent Peale: "Become a possibilitarian. No matter how dark things seem to be or actually are, raise your sights and see possibilities—always see them, for they're always there."

We are about to study one of the greatest possibilitarians of all time. His name is Joshua. Remember when he went as a spy into the promised land, how he saw the possibilities and brought back a good report? I have come to realize that being a possibilitarian requires courage and strength, two characteristics Joshua was blessed to have. "And Moses called unto Joshua, and said unto him in the sight of all Israel, Be strong and of a good courage: for thou must go with this people unto the land which the Lord hath sworn . . . to give them; and thou shalt cause them to inherit it. And the Lord, he it is that doth go before thee; he will be with thee, he will not fail thee, neither forsake thee: fear not, neither be dismayed" (Deuteronomy 31:7–8).

Did you know that the Lord counseled Joshua to be strong and of good courage six different times between Deuteronomy 31 and the first chapter of Joshua? Joshua teaches us that when you combine courage and strength with the companionship of the Lord, you can expect miracles—possibilities beyond your expectations.

In preparation for your introduction to Joshua, perhaps you could practice being a possibilitarian. As Elder F. Enzio Busche counseled: "Embrace this day with an enthusiastic welcome, no matter how it looks. The covenant with God to which you are true enables you to become enlightened by him, and nothing is impossible for you."[15] —EBF

Reflect and Respond

How could you raise your sights and discover the possibilities today?

Your favorite scripture in
Joshua 1

JOSHUA 2:18

Bind this line of **scarlet thread in the window.**

In this chapter, we learn of Rahab. I am intrigued that somewhere between the parting of the Red Sea and the moment when two spies from the house of Israel showed up on her doorstep, Rahab had come to know the Lord. This becomes clear in her conversation with the two spies, "For the Lord your God, he is God in heaven above, and in earth beneath" (Joshua 2:11).

Through the kindness of her actions in hiding them and sparing their lives, Rahab was promised a kindness from the spies—a promise that she would live through the destruction of Jericho. But that wasn't good enough for Rahab, who wanted that promise extended to "my father, and my mother, and my brethren, and my sisters" (Joshua 2:13). In order to make sure she and her family would be saved in the moment of destruction, the two spies instructed her, "Behold, when we come into the land, thou shalt bind this line of scarlet thread in the window which thou didst let us down by: and thou shalt bring thy father, and thy mother, and thy brethren, and all thy father's household, home unto thee" (Joshua 2:18).

My favorite symbol from this story is the scarlet thread hung in the window of Rahab's home. It reminds me of the lamb's blood carefully placed on each door in Egypt. The scarlet thread Rahab hung carefully in her window would serve as a reminder that her home was to be spared from the destruction. Passed over. Protected. Each of us needs a scarlet thread in our window, a reminder that just as Joshua saved Rahab, the Savior can save each of us. For me, that scarlet thread is found in taking the sacrament every week: a regular reminder that through the Atonement of Christ we experience saving, healing, and protection. —EBF

Reflect and Respond
How is the sacrament like a scarlet thread in your life?

Your favorite
scripture in
Joshua 2

JOSHUA 3:5

To morrow **the Lord will do
wonders among you.**

When Joshua gathered the people together next to the River Jordan, it was clear that they couldn't go back where they had come from, and yet there was a huge obstacle in front of them. What were they to do? In that period of waiting, Joshua gave clear instruction of how they would prepare for the miracle that would allow them to journey forward. He said, "Sanctify yourselves: for to morrow the Lord will do wonders among you" (Joshua 3:5). It was a point in their journey when they had to let the Lord lead, for they had not "passed this way heretofore" (Joshua 3:4). They had to trust Joshua and believe in a God who would do wonders in their behalf.

Joshua asked the priests to take up the ark of the covenant and walk before the people. Then Joshua told the priests to walk into the water carrying the ark and to stand still there. I try to imagine what kind of faith this must have required. I can picture those priests stepping into the river that was overflowing its banks because it was so full. Joshua told the people that if they watched, they would recognize that a living God was aware of them, and that He would deliver them "without fail" (Joshua 3:10).

I often wonder what thoughts filled their mind in that moment. Did they contemplate how they would cross that great expanse of water? It is so interesting that before the miracle could happen, their faith had to be made manifest with action. So they stepped into the water, *and then* the waters "stood and rose up upon an heap" and the priests "stood firm on *dry ground*" (Joshua 3:16–17; emphasis added). This is the process of sanctification: stepping in and standing still as we prepare for the Lord to work miracles in our own lives. —EBF

Reflect and Respond
What do stepping in and standing still look like in your life right now?

Your favorite scripture in
Joshua 3

JOSHUA 4:6

What mean ye by these stones?

After Joshua and his people had crossed the riverbed, the Lord told Joshua to have twelve men pick up twelve stones from the very middle of the river to use for a monument on the other side. I imagine that the journey across the river was quite a trek. These men probably had families and personal belongings they were required to move across. Now, as if they had not shouldered enough, they were asked to go back and carry an added burden. I am sure as they walked to the very middle of that riverbed, they questioned the Lord. *Could they not set up a monument with stones from the far side of the river and still remember the journey?*

But the Lord wanted stones from the midst of Jordan.

Once they had brought the twelve stones out of the riverbed, Joshua placed them together as a memorial. "And he spake unto the children of Israel, saying, When your children shall ask their fathers in time to come, saying, What mean these stones? Then ye shall let your children know, saying, Israel came over this Jordan on dry land. . . . That all the people of the earth might know the hand of the Lord, that it is mighty" (Joshua 4:21–24).

These twelve men left a legacy for generations to come of their testimony of the Lord and the great miracle of His hand in their life. Years later, when their children asked, "what mean ye by these stones?" (Joshua 4:6), these fathers would point to the river, full to overflowing its banks, and speak of a time when they had walked to its very middle on dry ground and carried those stones to the shore. In that moment, it would be their great privilege to testify of the miracles of the Lord. —EBF

Reflect and Respond

Think back over the miraculous moments in your own life. What are your twelve stones?

Your favorite
scripture in
Joshua 4

JOSHUA 5:13

Art thou for us?

Remember in Exodus 3 when the Lord appeared to Moses in a burning bush? There was a moment when Moses turned aside to look, and then he took off his shoes and stood on holy ground. This was the moment when Moses was introduced to the Lord, and the Lord promised to deliver Israel.

Many years later, when Joshua stood outside the walls of Jericho, Joshua lifted up his eyes to look and saw a man standing with his sword drawn in his hand. "Art thou for us, or for our adversaries?" he asked the stranger. The man said, "Nay; but as captain of the host of the Lord am I now come. And Joshua fell on his face to the earth, and did worship, and said unto him, What saith my lord unto his servant?" (Joshua 5:13–14). Suddenly this story becomes familiar, "And the captain of the Lord's host said unto Joshua, Loose thy shoe from off thy foot; for the place wheron thou standest is holy" (Joshua 5:15). And Joshua did.

Two prophets who turned aside to look. Two prophets who took off their shoes. Two prophets who learned what it is to stand on holy ground. On this, the eve of Jericho's victory, the Lord showed up again as the Deliverer, just as He had for Moses.

He will do the same for each of us. He will enter our stories, He will create holy ground, He will bring deliverance—but we must turn aside and look.

He is for us.

Perhaps He is just waiting for us to ask, *what saith my lord unto his servant?* —EBF

Reflect and Respond
What revelation have you experienced in holy places recently?

Your favorite scripture in
Joshua 5

JOSHUA 6:16

Shout; for the Lord hath given you the city.

Soon after arriving in the promised land, the children of Israel were engaged in a battle against the city of Jericho. The Lord commanded them to take the city, but the walls were high and impenetrable. When the children of Israel arrived, the whole city was closed tightly, with no one coming in or out. Have you ever faced closed, high walls before? Obstacles too tall for the likes of you?

The Lord's instructions to Joshua were rather unconventional and unexpected. The army of Israel was supposed to circle the city one time every day for six straight days. On the seventh day, they would walk around it again and again for a total of seven times. In the front of the army were seven trumpeters—priests who would carry ram's horns. Behind them, the ark of the covenant would be carried. On the seventh day, after the seventh revolution of the city, the priests would blast their trumpets, and then the whole army would shout! The Lord promised that if they followed that pattern, at the sound of the shout, the walls would come tumbling down and the Lord would give them the city. And so it went: the circles, the army, the ark, the trumpets, and the shout. Seven times, until the walls came down flat.

Some walls the Lord might expect us to climb, and others will take time to fall. We might feel like we are just going in circles. But if we are patient and follow His lead, eventually we will be led to shout, for God will give us the city. —DB

Reflect and Respond

When have you let out your shout of victory? When have those walls come tumbling down?

Your favorite scripture in
Joshua 6

JOSHUA 11:15

He left nothing undone.

We have a raspberry garden that requires caretaking. If we are not careful, it can be overtaken by weeds that will eventually choke out the raspberries completely.

Every spring, as we begin to weed the garden, the task at hand overwhelms us. We have to pay particular attention to every single weed. None can be left behind, not even the very small ones; the job requires that nothing be left undone. So, we pull out every weed, one by one, down to the roots, until none are left, so there is no chance of one small weed overtaking the raspberries.

The process reminds me of the description in the book of Joshua of how the people of Israel went to war against all of the cities in the promised land. "As the Lord commanded Moses his servant, so did Moses command Joshua, and so did Joshua; he *left nothing undone* of all that the Lord commanded Moses" (Joshua 11:15; emphasis added). He took all the land, and "Joshua made war *a long time* with all those kings" (Joshua 11:18; emphasis added). "The king of Jericho, one . . . the king of Jerusalem, one . . . the king of Makkedah, one" (Joshua 12: 9–10, 16). Joshua checked them off one by one as they were conquered completely—none left, so there would be no chance of Israel being overtaken. I have to be honest: I worried a little as I read these war chapters. Were the people that dangerous? Did the Israelites really have to destroy every single one?

The Book of Mormon provides the answer: "And after they had crossed the river Jordan he did make them mighty unto the driving out of the children of the land, yea, unto the scattering them to destruction. And now, do ye suppose that the children of this land, who were in the land of promise, who were driven out by our fathers, do ye suppose that they were righteous? Behold, I say unto you, Nay. . . . This people had rejected every word of God, and they were ripe in iniquity; and the fulness of the wrath of God was upon them; and the Lord did curse the land against them . . . unto their destruction" (1 Nephi 17:32–33, 35).

I consider the raspberry garden and realize that sometimes a very small weed can quickly overtake a very large garden. The Lord knows this, and He knows how to protect us against small things that could eventually destroy us. The people in the land could be compared to the sins of our lives. We can't just focus on the big ones, the dangerous ones. We have to remember to work on the little ones, even the ones that seem innocent. We must keep trying to conquer them until the day they are gone.

One day we will rest from this constant battle, but now we fight. It might take a long time, but we must leave nothing undone. The conquering will make us stronger. I love the passage in Joshua 14:11–12 when Caleb says, "As yet I am as strong this day as I was in the day that Moses sent me: as my strength was then, even so is my strength now, for war, both to go out, and to come in. Now therefore give me this mountain . . . the Lord will be with me." —EBF

Reflect and Respond

Is there anything in your life that has been left undone? How might you go about conquering it?

Your favorite scripture in **Joshua 11**

JOSHUA 24:22

We are witnesses.

In Joshua 24, Joshua gathered all the tribes of Israel with their elders, judges, and officers. He reminded them of their fathers who served other gods, idols who did not feel after them. Then he reminded them of the great blessings and miracles that had come when they had chosen to follow the Lord God of Israel. Joshua spoke of the flood, the birth of Isaac, and the plague in Egypt just before the Lord delivered them. He reminded them of the parting of the Red Sea, the wandering through the wilderness, and the fighting and possession of the land "for which ye did not labour, and cities which ye built not, and ye dwell in them." And then, after all these reminders, he counseled, "Now therefore fear the Lord, and *serve him in sincerity* and in truth: and put away the gods which your fathers served on the other side of the flood, and in Egypt; and serve ye the Lord" (Joshua 24:13–14; emphasis added).

What follows next is the familiar verse: "Choose you this day whom ye will serve . . . but as for me and my house, we will serve the Lord" (Joshua 24:15). And the people answered, "Therefore we will also serve the Lord; for he is our God" (Joshua 24:18).

There was a name given to those who chose to commit: "And Joshua said unto the people, Ye are witnesses against yourselves that ye have chosen you the Lord, to serve him. And they said, We are witnesses" (Joshua 24:22). Do you remember the times when you recognized the Lord's hand in your life? Have you covenanted to follow Him? Is it a choice you make daily?

This chapter extends the same invitation to each of us: choose the Lord. Become His witness. —EBF

Reflect and Respond

How have you chosen to stand as a witness?

Your favorite scripture in Joshua 24

JUDGES 2:16

**Nevertheless the Lord raised up
judges, which delivered them.**

The book of Judges begins with the death of Israel's leader, Joshua, and there was confusion about how to move forward. The command to clear the land of all the Canaanites was still unfulfilled, and the people of Israel were surrounded on every side by neighboring nations that would not be kind about having them there. The book of Judges seems to follow a pattern. Again and again, the children of Israel turned against the Lord and lost His divine protection. Because they were weak on their own, they were conquered by one of those neighboring nations and were forced to live as slaves. This continued until eventually the children of Israel repented of their stubborn and evil ways and cried to the Lord for deliverance. Despite their continued rebellion, each time they repented and asked for mercy, the Lord raised up a new judge (a leader or chief) to deliver them. This pattern continued year after year, judge after judge, throughout the entire book.

Each judge that was chosen by the Lord was a little unexpected. Each of them had a characteristic of weakness. In each story, it's as if the Lord was teaching the people that it would be through His strength that they would be delivered.

In the prologue chapter of the book of Judges, my favorite word is *nevertheless.* When you read this book, you might think the Lord should have given up on Israel. You may think they have run out of chances, and you might be perplexed about how they can keep falling into the same problem again and again. *Nevertheless,* the Lord still continued to raise up judges to deliver them. That gives a rebellious soul like me a lot of hope. —DB

Reflect and Respond

Have you ever experienced a similar pattern to the book of Judges in your own story?

Your favorite
scripture in
Judges 2

JUDGES 4:8

If thou wilt go with me, then I will go.

In chapter 4 of Judges we meet two great women. The first is "Deborah, a prophetess, the wife of Lapidoth, she judged Israel at that time" (Judges 4:4). Cassel, a Bible scholar, explains that the term "wife of Lapidoth" could also have been translated in Hebrew to read "a woman of torch-like spirit."[16] *Deborah, a prophetess, a woman of torch-like spirit, she judged Israel at that time.* That is the way I like to envision Deborah. No wonder the children of Israel came up to be judged by her as she sat under the palm tree in mount Ephraim. I am sure the spirit that she carried was inviting and wise. The scriptures teach that her spirit also prompted courage.

On the day that Deborah persuaded Barak to gather his army to fight against Sisera, who had nine hundred chariots of iron, Barak had only one request, "If thou wilt go with me, then I will go: but if thou wilt not go with me, then I will not go. And she said, I will surely go with thee" (Judges 4:8–9). Deborah's torch-like spirit had the power to instill courage in others and to inspire them to follow the command of the Lord.

When Barak came to Deborah for wisdom and encouragement, she prophesied that Sisera, the enemy to Israel, would be delivered into the hand of a woman. As the battle grew more intense and Sisera saw that he was close to being defeated, he escaped. When he ran for cover, he found the tent of the second great woman in this chapter: Jael, the wife of Heber. She came out to meet him and offered him safety in her home. He was weary from the fighting, so she covered him with a blanket, gave him a drink of milk, and told him she would stand guard at the front door while he slept.

After Sisera had fallen asleep, Jael slowly crept through the tent and with a hammer and a nail ended Sisera's life and the misery of Israel. When Barak came near, Jael called him into the tent to see how Israel had been delivered by the hand of a woman.

The Lord used two women to save Israel on that day, and, from the looks of things, two very different women. One of them was well-known and wise, with leadership and battle skills. The other one was at home alone in her tent, quietly going about her work with a different kind of skill set. But together, these two women served as instruments in the hand of the Lord to win the day. The Lord used both of their individual strengths to bring about His purposes.

After the army was defeated and Israel was delivered, Deborah and Barak sang a song of praise. One verse of this song contains a sentence that is profound, "I Deborah arose, that I arose a mother in Israel" (Judges 5:7). A mother in Israel delivered the people from bondage.

Have you ever taken the time to ponder how many mothers in Israel have been part of the process of deliverance throughout the generations of time? Mary, the mother of Jesus. Elizabeth. The mother of Moses. Hannah, Samuel's mother. What about the mothers of the stripling warriors? Sometimes we question the worth of women in the Lord's plan. The stories of Deborah and Jael speak loud and clear in this regard: never underestimate the power of a righteous woman. —DB and EBF

Reflect and Respond

Consider women you know. What different gifts do they have that enable them to do God's work?

Your favorite scripture in
Judges 4

JUDGES 6:14

**Go in this thy might, and thou shalt save
Israel . . . have not I sent thee?**

Just as they had done before and would do again, Israel turned their back on the Lord, lost His divine protection, and were conquered by their neighbors—the Midianites this time. For seven long years, they lived in caves and watched the Midianites take everything from them. And then they turned back and cried to God for deliverance. In answer to their plea, the Lord sent Gideon.

"The Lord is with thee, thou mighty man of valour" (Judges 6:12). Those were the first words the angel called out to Gideon when he found him hiding behind the winepress. I imagine Gideon looking over his shoulder, wondering who the angel was talking to. Certainly it couldn't be him. He was no mighty man of valour. But the angel addressed him as the person he *could* be, not the one he thought he was. He would be on the Lord's errand, and the Lord in His strength would go with him.

But Gideon couldn't see it. He hesitated with fear. He didn't match up to the mission. He asked for a sign from the Lord. I imagine it was not to verify his own plans, but to be sure of God's. He laid out a fleece of wool next to his bed at night and asked the Lord to let the dew fall only on the fleece and not the floor around it. In the morning, he twisted the fleece, filling a bowl full of water, and the ground was dry. That day, Gideon didn't learn *how* he would carry out his mission, but he did learn that God was in it, nudging him forward. He would still have to take many trusting steps into the dark. However, despite Gideon's fears and inadequacies, the Lord confirmed to him what he could be and do on His errand. —DB

Reflect and Respond
When have you felt God nudge you forward?

Your favorite
scripture in
Judges 6

JUDGES 7:17

Look on me, and do likewise.

Gideon, one of God's heroes, mighty man of valour, considered himself the least in his father's house. Was it his humility that allowed the Lord to mold him into the hero he was meant to become? On the day of the battle, Gideon rose up early and prepared his army. "And the Lord said unto Gideon, The people that are with thee are too many" (Judges 7:2). The first group that was asked to leave were those who were fearful and afraid, those who did not trust the Lord and His power. Ten thousand remained. Still the Lord told Gideon, "The people are yet too many; bring them down unto the water, and I will try them for thee there" (Joshua 7:4). According to Alfred Edersheim: "If we ask about the rationale of this means of distinction, we conclude, of course, that it indicated the bravest and most ardent warriors, who would not stoop to kneel, but hastily quenched their thirst out of the hollow of their hands, in order to hasten to battle."[17]

Now, after this final test, only three hundred men remained. This last three hundred would face the camp of Midian, 135,000 people strong. Talk about trusting the Lord. But even more astounding was the way Gideon prepared his warriors for the battle. Their weaponry consisted of a trumpet, a pitcher, and a lamp. His counsel to them was clear, "Look on me, and do likewise . . . as I do, so shall ye do" (Judges 7:17). What did Gideon do? Trust.

In the moment of battle, those three hundred men focused on Gideon, one of God's heroes, a man who had proven the Lord, who trusted the Lord implicitly. The warriors focused on him, "and they stood every man in his place" (Judges 7:21). —EBF

Reflect and Respond

How have you learned to trust the Lord?

Your favorite scripture in **Judges 7**

JUDGES 16:28

**O Lord God, remember me, I pray thee,
and strengthen me, I pray thee, only this once.**

The story of Samson might be one of the most adventurous, memorable, and epic stories in the whole Old Testament. In a time when Israel needed another deliverer, the Lord chose Samson. He was different from the rest of the deliverers in the book of Judges, who were all underqualified and found strength in their weakness. Samson was mighty and gifted from the outset. In contrast to the others, he actually became weak because of his strength.

Although he was successful in bringing down the Philistines, the enemy to Israel at the time, Samson did it by pursuing his own wishes and desires. He was vengeful, prideful, and lustful, and did not seek to follow the counsel or ways of the Lord. His acts of strength were amazing, but none of them were admirable.

Eventually, his trust in his own strength led to his downfall. After a lifetime of doing what was right in his own eyes, ironically, when Samson was caught by the Philistines, he lost his eyesight—and that was when he began to truly see. As he was chained up in the temple of the Philistines and heard the mocking cries of the enemy against the Lord, Samson cried, perhaps for the first time, to *God* for strength. In his moment of weakness, he looked to heaven.

"Only this once," he prayed, "strengthen me." And God did. It took Samson many years to learn the lesson. But once he found strength in the Lord (and it only took once for it to happen), he finally became the deliverer God chose him to be. —DB

Reflect and Respond

How do we keep our strengths from blinding us to what God could be doing in our life?

Your favorite scripture in
Judges 16

RUTH 2:11

It hath fully been shewed me, **all that thou hast done** unto thy mother in law.

The end of Judges is filled with wickedness, images we don't want to think about, and experiences that make us question why it is so hard for people to remember and to choose God. In the midst of all the stories of wickedness, do you ever wonder to yourself, *wasn't there anyone who knew what it was to be true?* But then we turn the page and discover Ruth. As you read her story, perhaps you could focus on the descriptions of Ruth: a woman of virtue in the midst of gross wickedness.

"And Ruth said, Entreat me not to leave thee, or to return from following after thee: for whither thou goest, I will go; and where thou lodgest, I will lodge: thy people shall be my people, and thy God my God" (Ruth 1:16).

"She was steadfastly minded" (Ruth 1:18).

"Blessed be thou of the Lord, my daughter: for thou hast shewed more kindness in the latter end than at the beginning" (Ruth 3:10).

"For all the city of my people doth know that thou art a virtuous woman" (Ruth 3:11).

Ruth was a woman who had learned to look to the Lord with a heart full of hope, even when it seemed as if hope was gone, a woman who loved so deeply that loyalty wasn't a decision but rather a consequence of that love. Because of that, it was said of her, "The Lord recompense thy work, and a *full reward* be given thee of the Lord God of Israel, under whose wings thou art come to trust" (Ruth 2:12; emphasis added). May our lives lead us to know the Lord God of Israel, under whose wings we too can come to trust. —EBF

....

Reflect and Respond

What is your favorite characteristic of Ruth?

Your favorite scripture in Ruth 1–2

RUTH 3:17

Go not empty unto thy mother in law.

Out of all the themes in the book of Ruth, the transition from empty to full is my favorite. We see this principle taught best through Naomi, Ruth's mother-in-law. After her husband had passed away, after Orpah returned to her mother's house, after Ruth had accompanied her all the way back to her homeland, Naomi decided to change her name. "She said unto them, Call me not Naomi," which means sweet, "call me Mara," which means bitter. For, she said, "the Almighty hath dealt very bitterly with me. I went out full, and the Lord hath brought me home again empty" (Ruth 1:20–21). She was in a devastating place, a place devoid of blessing. But the Lord hadn't forgotten Naomi. It was through Ruth that her fulness would be found again—a woman who was not her own blood, not even from her own culture or religion, but whose heart had been given to Naomi's God. Through Ruth the blessing would come. Boaz spoke of it first: "The Lord recompense thy work, and a *full* reward be given thee of the Lord God of Israel" (Ruth 2:12; emphasis added). Then Boaz told Ruth to return to her mother-in-law, saying, "Go not empty unto thy mother in law" (Ruth 3:17).

In chapter four, the writer mentions three women: Ruth and Leah, who were barren, and Tamar, whose father-in-law stood in the way of her having a family. The Lord redeemed all of those situations. The promise is clear: He can take barren and empty places and make them full.

When Ruth had her first son, the women said unto Naomi, "Blessed be the Lord, which hath not left thee this day without . . . and he shall be unto thee a restorer of thy life, and a nourisher of thine old age" (Ruth 4:14–15). From empty to full. Blessed by the Lord. —EBF

Reflect and Respond

When have you experienced going from empty to full?

Your favorite scripture in
Ruth 3–4

1 SAMUEL 1:27

For this child I prayed.

When Hannah approached the Lord, the scriptures tell us it was out of an abundance of grief. Her overwhelming sadness is described as a bitterness of soul. She wept sore, prayed, and did not eat as she prepared to petition the Lord. Finally, after all her preparation, and after many years of waiting, Hannah pled to the Lord for the blessing of a child, promising that she would give that child to the Lord all the days of his life. Hannah pled with the Lord, and He answered through His prophet, "Go in peace: and the God of Israel grant thee thy petition that thou hast asked of him" (1 Samuel 1:17).

Think of Hannah walking out of the temple that day. The scriptures tell us that she "went her way, and did eat, and her countenance was no more sad" (1 Samuel 1:18). This is not a description of what doubt looks like, it's what faith looks like, even after years of praying and hoping and petitioning for the same blessing over and over again. This time, after Hannah petitioned the Lord, the scriptures tell us, "the Lord remembered her" (1 Samuel 1:19). Every time I read this sentence, my testimony of God's love is increased. I know that because He remembered Hannah in her abundance of grief, He will remember me. I know not when the blessing will come, but I know I will not be forgotten of the Lord. In time, Hannah bore a son, "and called his name Samuel, saying, Because I have asked him of the Lord" (1 Samuel 1:20).

When Samuel was very young, Hannah took him to Eli, the prophet, and lent him to the Lord as she had promised. "And she said, O my lord, as thy soul liveth, my lord, I am the woman that stood by thee here, praying unto the Lord. *For this child I prayed; and the Lord hath given me my petition which I asked of him*" (1 Samuel 1:26–27; emphasis added).

For this child I prayed . . .

I can't imagine how hard it must have been to entrust the tiny child that she had longed for into the hands of someone else to be raised, to give up the blessing she had yearned for after such a short time. But the story does not speak of sadness; instead,

Hannah bears testimony of the goodness of God, saying, "My heart rejoiceth in the Lord. . . . There is none holy as the Lord: for there is none beside thee: neither is there any rock like our God" (1 Samuel 2:1–2). Through the waiting, the grief, the bitterness, the tears, the petitioning, and even through the blessing, Hannah had come to know the Lord. Perhaps Samuel, this gift from the Lord, might be labeled as a blessing come late. But have you ever considered that the answer to her prayer that day in the temple might not have been the greatest blessing Hannah received? Maybe Hannah's greatest blessing was what came as a result of the waiting, the petitioning, the grief, because through the process the Savior had become her rock. Could that have been the greater blessing?

In the years that followed, even though Samuel was not with her, Hannah remembered her precious gift from the Lord. She spent countless hours sewing for her son. Once every year she visited the beloved child that she had pled for and brought him what must have surely been a token of her love. Samuel tells us, "Moreover his mother made him a little coat, and brought it to him from year to year" (1 Samuel 2:19). Right away we know how important each of those little coats must have been to Samuel. If they hadn't been, he wouldn't have remembered to write them into the history of his life. Do you wonder if Samuel wore each of those coats and thought of his mother's prayers, which resulted in the miracle of his life? —EBF

Reflect and Respond

What are you praying for right now? What can you learn from Hannah?

Your favorite scripture in 1 Samuel 1

1 SAMUEL 3:7

Now Samuel did not yet know the Lord.

Samuel spent his days as a boy serving the Lord and assisting Eli the high priest in the temple. One night, the "Lord called Samuel"—and woke him up. Samuel thought it was Eli who called him, and he rushed to Eli's room to ask him what he needed. Eli told him, I didn't call you, go back to bed. And so he did, but then the voice came again, "Samuel." So, Samuel got up a second time and went to Eli's room. Now both of them must have been so confused. Then the story says, "Now Samuel did not yet know the Lord" (1 Samuel 3:4–7). He didn't recognize His voice, because he didn't know it. When the Lord called Samuel a third time, he still didn't know the Lord, but Eli realized what was happening, and he told the boy, "Go, lie down: and it shall be, if he call thee, that thou shalt say, Speak, Lord; for thy servant heareth" (1 Samuel 3:9). And it happened exactly as Eli said it would.

This would be the first of many experiences Samuel would have with the Lord in his life—a Lord he did not know *yet*. I love that little word in that verse. He did not *yet* know the Lord, but that didn't disqualify him from being called and being used as the Lord's servant to do a great work. A word like *yet* might come across as a negative. It might sound to us as if he was behind where he should have been. But I think there is a lot of thrill in the word *yet*. It means that anything is around the corner and everything is a possibility. It also means that God isn't afraid to call those who are "not yet." —DB

Reflect and Respond

What are some things you hope for that have not developed or come about quite "yet"?

Your favorite scripture in 1 Samuel 3

1 SAMUEL 7:12

**Then Samuel took a stone . . .
and called the name of it Eben-ezer.**

Several decades ago, I was asked to accompany a friend who was singing a solo at a missionary homecoming. The song was "Come, Thou Fount of Every Blessing." I hate to admit it, but some of the words just didn't make any sense to my friend and me, particularly the phrase, "Here I raise my Ebenezer; Here by Thy great help I've come." We had no idea who or what Ebenezer was, so we changed that part of the song and left out the line entirely. After the meeting, the missionary thanked us for the song. "But," he said, "you left out my very favorite part." We told him it was because the line didn't make sense to us and asked him what the meaning was. With a smile he invited us to take a look at the seventh chapter of First Samuel.

Just as each of the prophets had done before him, there came a moment when Samuel asked Israel to put away their strange gods and turn to the Lord. This time it was so that they could be delivered from the Philistines. Samuel asked them to "Prepare your hearts unto the Lord, and serve him only: and he will deliver you" (1 Samuel 7:3). Israel was afraid, and they said to Samuel, "Cease not to cry unto the Lord our God for us, that he will save us. . . . And Samuel cried unto the Lord for Israel; and the Lord heard him" (1 Samuel 7:8–9). And Israel prevailed. Here comes the important part, "Then Samuel took a stone . . . and called the name of it Eben-ezer, saying, Hitherto hath the Lord helped us" (1 Samuel 7:12). If you look at the footnote for *Eben-ezer* you will find that the name means "the stone of help."

The stone became a memorial for Israel of a time when the Lord had helped them through a situation they could not have made it through on their own. —EBF

Reflect and Respond

Do you have an Ebenezer? A reminder of a time when the Lord helped you?

Your favorite
scripture in
1 Samuel 7

1 SAMUEL 8:19-20

**We will have a king over us;
that we also may be like all the nations.**

After many years as Israel's judge, Samuel began to get older, and he appointed his sons to be judges and rulers over the people after him. Unfortunately, they were not like their father; they took bribes and had horrible judgment. So all of the elders gathered together and came to Samuel and asked him to appoint a king to rule over the tribes of Israel instead. Samuel knew right away it wasn't a good idea, but he went to the Lord to seek His guidance. When he returned, he listed for the people all of the heartache and trouble that would come into their lives if they had a king. Their sons and daughters would become servants to a king's selfish wishes. They would be taxed heavily and eventually lose their freedom. Despite all the prophet's many arguments and predictions about what would happen, the people refused to listen and demanded a king.

"We will have a king over us; that we also may be like all the nations" (1 Samuel 8:19–20). When the Lord brought the children of Israel out of Egypt and into their promised land, His hope was they would be His representatives and teach and spread the rescue of God and be a blessing to all other nations. But instead of Israel influencing the other nations, the other nations started to influence Israel. They wanted a king so they could be like everybody else. But that is not who they were called to be. They were called to be peculiar—to live after the manner of holiness, with God as their king.

In order to change the world, we must certainly live in it, but we can never live like it. —DB

Reflect and Respond
What does it look like to live among all the nations but to not be like those nations?

Your favorite
scripture in
1 Samuel 8

1 SAMUEL 10:6

**And the Spirit of the Lord will come upon thee, and
thou . . . shalt be turned into another man.**

After the people of Israel ignored Samuel's advice against having a king, the Lord
consented and told Samuel to go ahead and find one. If Israel wanted a king, the Lord
would be the one to choose who it would be. The moment that Samuel saw Saul, the
son of Kish, the Lord whispered into Samuel's heart that he, Saul, was to be the leader
and king of His people. Saul had a reputation for being a good man. When Samuel and
Saul met, it was because some of Saul's father's donkeys had been lost. He had been out
looking for them when one of Saul's servants told him about a holy prophet that lived in
the place where they were, and Saul went to find him. Little did Saul know how inspired
that advice would turn out to be. When they met, the Lord said, "Behold the man whom
I spake to thee of! this same shall reign over my people" (1 Samuel 9:17).

Saul saw himself that day as a donkey keeper—nothing more. But God saw a king's
heart. As Saul protested against the idea, Samuel made promises to him about his new
role. "The Spirit of the Lord will come upon thee, and thou . . . shalt be turned into
another man" (1 Samuel 10:6). This was a calling that Saul would grow into. Under the
influence of the Spirit, he would become who God needed him to become. He was a
good man already, but God had something even greater for him.

As Saul left his conversation with Samuel, perhaps contemplating his most unusual
day, "God gave him another heart" (1 Samuel 10:9) and fit him for the days ahead. —DB

Reflect and Respond

*When have you experienced God giving you another heart—
changing you into a new person?*

Your favorite
scripture in
1 Samuel 10

1 SAMUEL 17:29

Is there not a cause?

I bet if we did a survey of people's favorite Bible stories, we would find the tale of the young Bethlehemite defeating a giant near the top. The story is thick with the heroism of youth, the courage of the faithful, and the mighty delivering power of the God of Israel.

The battle fought in the valley of Elah was no ordinary battle. This valley was one of Israel's final defensive strongholds. As part of an ancient custom of war, and as a way to preserve troops, the winner of this battle would be decided by a duel of champions. Goliath, at over nine feet tall, and with armor weighing over 150 pounds, was an easy selection to fight for the Philistines, but "all the men of Israel, when they saw the man, fled from him, and were sore afraid" (1 Samuel 17:24). Then David showed up, with his classic question, "Is there not a cause?" (1 Samuel 17:29). With this faithful exclamation, David volunteered to fight Goliath.

Saul was hesitant, but David, the young shepherd boy, grabbed his sling and five smooth stones from a nearby brook. As he approached Goliath, David returned the taunts with this powerful rebuttal: "Thou comest to me with a sword, and with a spear, and with a shield: but I come to thee in the name of the Lord of hosts" (1 Samuel 17:45). Then he *ran* to meet the Philistine. We know what happened next. I imagine there was silence in the valley for just a moment as a confirmation settled on each heart that there was indeed a God in Israel, and then a cheer. God had prevailed through a young shepherd boy.

Each of us will find ourselves in the valley of Elah with moments of fear to overcome and impossible tasks ahead. We must have courage, like David, to stand for our cause. —DB

Reflect and Respond
What is your cause?

Your favorite
scripture in
1 Samuel 17

1 SAMUEL 20:17

And Jonathan caused David to swear again, because he loved him: for he loved him as he loved his own soul.

After David slew Goliath in the battle of Elah, his popularity grew rapidly in Israel. Everyone sang and cheered over David, and it made King Saul wildly jealous. From that day forward, Saul sought to kill David and thus get rid of someone he saw as a competitor. Perhaps he would have been successful if it hadn't been for the protecting and watchful care of Jonathan, Saul's son and David's best friend.

Under the typical order of things, the king after Saul should have been Jonathan, his son and rightful heir. But before David went into battle with Goliath, he was chosen and anointed by Samuel the prophet to be the next king of Israel. There would have been a lot of motivation for Jonathan to not look after and protect David, especially if he himself wanted to be king. But he did it anyway. The Old Testament talks about their friendship as a covenant one. A covenant relationship is one in which people put the friendship above their own individual wants and needs. It is an "us" over "me" type of relationship. It is a relationship you stay in, even if it is hard or inconvenient. Jonathan loved David like the truest of friends.

In one powerful encounter between the two men (see 1 Samuel 18:4), Jonathan takes off his robe, his royal vestments, and his sword and gives them to David. To David, this would have been a sign of Jonathan handing over his crown, life, and allegiance to his friend and future king. Jonathan loved David and the Lord's will more than he loved his own life and the chance to be king himself. —DB

Reflect and Respond
Who do you know who is a friend like Jonathan?

Your favorite scripture in
1 Samuel 20

1 SAMUEL 25:28

Forgive the trespass of thine handmaid.

In the midst of the drama of First and Second Samuel is an often-overlooked type of Christ. Her name is Abigail, "a woman of good understanding, and of a beautiful countenance" (1 Samuel 25:3), wife of a rude and hard man named Nabal. Nabal kept his flocks near the fields where David and his men had been staying. David's army had helped to protect the sheep and their shepherds while they had camped there. One morning, David found they were short on food, so he sent messengers to request small amounts of provision from Nabal's abundance. Nabal rebuked the men with insults and sent them away empty. In a moment demanding justice, David ordered half of his men to grab their swords and accompany him to confront Nabal.

Aware of her husband's bitter nature and the approaching army, Abigail gathered provisions and embarked to intercept an angry David and protect an undeserving Nabal. When Abigail came up to the soldiers, she fell to the feet of David in a humble bow, "Upon me, my lord, upon me let this iniquity be. . . . I pray thee, forgive the trespass of thine handmaid" (1 Samuel 25:24, 28). Here, a woman of perfect grace stands between two guilty parties, having done no wrong herself, but taking the full responsibility. *Forgive me. Blame me. Direct your anger at my innocence.* In that moment, David's heart melted, and peace was restored.

I am reminded of the Savior pleading our case before the Father for a crime He hasn't committed. We've all been on one side or the other. Most of the time I am a Nabal. Sometimes I am a David. Always, He is my Abigail. —DB

Reflect and Respond

How do you feel about the Savior interceding and pleading in your behalf?

Your favorite scripture in
1 Samuel 25

1 SAMUEL 30:19

David recovered all.

Have you ever experienced a riptide? This current is so powerful it can drag a swimmer standing waist-deep out into deeper waters. Sometimes a swimmer caught in a riptide will die from the exhaustion of trying to swim back to shore. This is why lifeguards are placed on duty. They are always watching for signs of danger, listening for a cry for help, standing ready in an instant to pursue. Their goal is to recover all, to lose none.

David knew what it was to be a rescuer. When the Amalekites invaded, they took the women captive, both great and small. The people wept and lifted up their voices. "And David was greatly distressed; . . . but David encouraged himself in the Lord his God" (1 Samuel 30:6). He enquired after the Lord, "Shall I pursue?" And the Lord answered, "Pursue: for thou shalt . . . without fail recover all" (1 Samuel 30:8).

So David went to rescue what was his. As they approached the Amalekites, they must have felt the power of the danger ahead, for the people were "spread abroad upon all the earth" (1 Samuel 30:16). But still David pressed forward and led the rescue. "And David recovered all that the Amalekites had carried away . . . and there was nothing lacking to them, neither small nor great, neither sons nor daughters, neither spoil, nor any thing that they had taken to them: David recovered all" (1 Samuel 30:18–19). The wives. The children. The small. The great.

Within the story of David, we see a reminder of the Savior. A lifeguard. A lifesaver. A rescuer. One whose vigil is constant. Always He is listening. Always He hears the cry for help. His arms are outstretched constantly. He has promised to rescue us, every one. To recover all. —EBF

Reflect and Respond

How have you experienced the Savior as a rescuer?

Your favorite scripture in 1 Samuel 30

2 SAMUEL 6:14

David danced before the Lord with all his might.

In a brief break from the war with the Philistines, thirty thousand people gathered to the city of David. Musicians lined the streets, playing instruments of all types as the ark was marched to its resting place in the city center. As the procession moved through the streets, David began to offer sacrifices unto the Lord, receiving the ark into the city with gladness. Now comes my favorite part—almost as quickly as he began playing music and offering his sacrifices, "David danced before the Lord with all his might" (2 Samuel 6:14). The festivities ended with more sacrifices being offered and a fancy feast provided by David for all of those in attendance.

When David returned home, he was met with a rebuke from Michal, who had seen him "leaping and dancing before the Lord." She snidely remarked, "How glorious was the king of Israel to day, who uncovered himself . . . as one of the vain fellows shamelessly uncovereth himself" (2 Samuel 6:20). This was because when David began dancing, he had removed his kingly robes—ancient symbols of dignity and power—to show his recognition of the true King of Israel. Michal had thought this was unfitting. David's response: "It was before the Lord, which chose me before thy father, and before all his house, to appoint me ruler over the people of the Lord, over Israel: therefore will I play before the Lord" (2 Samuel 6:21).

I have been thinking, what has the Lord done for me that causes me to say, *therefore I will play before the Lord*? In what ways can I show my praise, and adoration, and honor for a God worthy of feasts, music, dancing, standing, singing, praising, and shouts of hosanna? Today I will praise with all my might. —DB

Reflect and Respond
In what ways could you offer your own praises today?

Your favorite scripture in 2 Samuel 6

2 SAMUEL 9:11

As for Mephibosheth, said the king, **he shall eat at my table, as one of the king's sons.**

We meet Mephibosheth for the first time in 2 Samuel 4. He was the son of Jonathan and the grandson of King Saul. When the kingdom was under attack at the battle of Mount Gilboa, both Jonathan and King Saul were killed. Mephibosheth's nurse grabbed the five-year-old boy and fled. In her haste, he fell and was lame for the rest of his life.

When David became the king, he conquered the Philistines, took the ark to the city of David, and offered a prayer of thanksgiving. Then, he asked if there was anyone from Jonathan's family who was still alive because he wanted to show them the kindness of God. After inquiring, David found out about Jonathan's boy, who was lame. Immediately David sent for him, from Lo-debar, considered one of the poorest towns in Gilead.

"Now when Mephibosheth, the son of Jonathan, the son of Saul, was come unto David, he fell on his face, and did reverence . . . and David said unto him, Fear not: for I will surely shew thee kindness for Jonathan thy father's sake, and will restore thee all the land of Saul thy father; and thou shalt eat bread at my table continually" (2 Samuel 9:6–7).

Again, we see David as a type of Christ. Consider the lessons here. He sought one who had been cast out, who was in need of healing, looking for him in the least of the cities. He restored his land and family status and offered him a place at his table, not as a servant but as a son.

It is a beautiful story of redemption, of restoration, of saving. A reminder of the true role of the Master of the kingdom, to show the kindness of God. —EBF

Reflect and Respond
What is your favorite lesson from the story of Mephibosheth?

Your favorite scripture in 2 Samuel 9

2 SAMUEL 11:1

**At the time when kings go forth to battle . . .
David tarried still at Jerusalem.**

When David was on the battlefield, he was strong and victorious. He was with the Lord. You may remember that as he ran toward Goliath, he called out to the giant that he had come in "the name of the Lord of hosts, the God of the armies of Israel" (1 Samuel 17:45). But in a later time when kings went forth to battle, David stayed home—alone. He stopped battling.

What happened when David stayed home is one of the tragic stories of the Bible. It was a day when another kind of giant took down the king—the giant of lies and lust. One evening, David saw another man's wife bathing and called her to himself. The woman, Bathsheba, became pregnant, but instead of confessing his wrongs and acting as a king should act, David used his power and influence to try to hide the sin. He called Bathsheba's husband, Uriah, home from the battle to stage a cover-up. After a conversation, he sent Uriah home with a meal and gifts and an encouragement to spend the evening with his wife. Instead, in the morning, they found Uriah sleeping on the front porch. When David asked why he hadn't gone to his own bed, Uriah replied that he could not sleep comfortably when his friends were suffering in war.

Perhaps Uriah's words could have reminded David what it meant to live nobly and righteously. If only David had followed Uriah's example, perhaps further disaster could have been avoided. Instead, Uriah was placed on the front lines and killed.

Ironically, from the line of David and Bathsheba, the truest king of all kings would one day be born. One who came forth to battle for our wrongs, to help us overcome our giants—even when it feels undeserved. —DB

Reflect and Respond

*What is one thing that you are battling for in your life right now
that you should not give up on?*

Your favorite
scripture in
2 Samuel 11

2 SAMUEL 20:19

**Thou seekest to destroy . . .
a mother in Israel: why . . . ?**

In this chapter we read about a woman whose name is not given; she is simply referred to as a wise woman. As Joab and his army surrounded the walls of the city of Abel, I wonder if all the people took refuge inside their homes—everyone, except this woman. She walked out to meet Joab, who was armed for battle and intent on destroying the entire city in his pursuit of a wicked foe, Sheba. "Hear, hear; say, I pray you," she called. "Come near hither, that I may speak with thee" (2 Samuel 20:16).

I love the way she introduced herself: "I am one of them that are peaceable and faithful in Israel" (2 Samuel 20:19). She gave not a name but a description that inspired honor and admiration, and then she asked courageously: "Thou seekest to destroy a city and a mother in Israel: why . . . ?" (2 Samuel 20:19). Joab explained that it was not his desire to destroy, but that there was an evil man within the city walls who "hath lifted up his hand against the king" (2 Samuel 20:21). He must be delivered in order for the city to be saved. "Then the woman went unto all the people in her wisdom. And they cut off the head of Sheba the son of Bichri, and cast it out to Joab. And he . . . retired from the city" (2 Samuel 20:22).

The answer this wise woman teaches is that together we must be watchful. We cannot allow that which is evil or threatens our belief in our King to find a haven within our communities. We must become wise women in our cities, peaceable and faithful, strong in our beliefs, courageous enough to stand up and protect all that we love, and willing to cast out that which could bring us harm. —EBF

Reflect and Respond

How can you be wise about protecting your community, your home, and your family?

Your favorite
scripture in
2 Samuel 20

2 SAMUEL 23:8

**These be the names of the
mighty men whom David had . . .**

When my boys were in high school, I attended many lacrosse games. It was serious business. The athletes gathered with one purpose in mind: victory. They prepared hard for those games—the kind of preparing that takes place day after day, week after week, month after month. In lacrosse, the best of the best all have something in common—they have a right-hand *and* a left-hand shot. You are not born with that kind of talent. You earn it. These boys shot at a goal until the last light of sun faded, emptying buckets of balls, then gathering them back up from all across the field and emptying the bucket again. Again. Again.

These athletes remind me of the army that gathered to David's side. Their account is recorded in 1 Chronicles 12 and in 2 Samuel 23. These thirty-seven mighty men of valor were men who had prepared day after day, week after week, month after month. They were the elite from every tribe of Israel. What set them apart was their dedication, their diligence, their determination. "And they were among the mighty men, helpers of the war. They were armed with bows, *and could use both the right hand and the left* in hurling stones and shooting arrows out of a bow" (1 Chronicles 12:1–2; emphasis added). I can't help but wonder if these men shot their arrows until the last light of sun faded behind the mountain, if they hurled stones until their arms become so sore they could barely even lift them. Again. Again. Again. I love what these men said to David as they came to fortify his army, "Thine are we, David, and on thy side" (1 Chronicles 12:18). These were David's mighty men of valor. "They were not of double heart . . . all these men of war . . . came with a perfect heart . . . and all . . . were of one heart" (1 Chronicles 12:33, 38). —EBF

Reflect and Respond

How do you practice being on the Lord's side?

Your favorite
scripture in
2 Samuel 23

2 SAMUEL 24:24

**Neither will I offer burnt offerings unto the Lord my
God of that which doth cost me nothing.**

In a somewhat odd story in the life of King David, the Lord was upset with him for something he had done. It is difficult to determine exactly what it was, but in consequence a great plague came through the entire army. For a few days, many people suffered from the plague. David, in a way that seemed to foreshadow his future ancestor Jesus, went before the Lord and pleaded for and on behalf of his people. *Take me instead,* David petitioned. *Spare my brethren.*

Gad, a seer of the Lord, came to David and instructed him to build an altar of sacrifice. The place where he would build it was the threshing floor of Araunah the Jebusite. Interestingly, this would also be the place that one day the temple would be built in Jerusalem. When David came to the threshing floor, Araunah bowed down before David, shocked that a king would come and visit him. When David asked to buy the area to build an altar, Araunah offered it all to David for free—the floor, the materials for an altar and fire, and the oxen for the sacrifice. As kind or loyal as that was, David refused. He explained to the humble man that he would not offer up a sacrifice to his God "of that which doth cost me nothing." David understood that a sacrifice was only a sacrifice if it came at a cost. The price paid is what makes a sacrifice both powerful and exalting. It is where the love is.

Somewhere near that same spot, Jesus the King would come and offer up Himself as the ultimate sacrifice. This sacrifice that would cost Him everything would be ultimately powerful, everlastingly exalting, and the greatest manifestation of love the world would ever know. —DB

Reflect and Respond
What kind of impact has the offering of a sacrifice had on your heart?

Your favorite
scripture in
2 Samuel 24

1 KINGS 2:1

**Now the days of David drew nigh . . . and
he charged Solomon his son . . .**

As we start into the books of Kings, you will discover we also quote from the books of Chronicles. These books are similar to the four gospels in the New Testament—a retelling of the same story from two different perspectives. After gathering everything that would be needed to build the temple, David spoke with his son Solomon. "Then David gave to Solomon his son the pattern . . . all this, said David, the Lord made me understand in writing by his hand upon me, even all the works of this pattern" (1 Chronicles 28:11, 19). Besides the pattern, David gave his son some advice, "the Lord searcheth all hearts, and understandeth all the imaginations of the thoughts" (1 Chronicles 28:9). I try to comprehend the Lord's ability to understand my imaginations, and then I remember His role as creator and the imagination that must have taken. I love the last counsel that David gives to his son, "Take heed now; for the Lord hath chosen thee to build an house for the sanctuary: be strong, and do it" (1 Chronicles 28:10).

What has the Lord chosen you to do? When He searches your heart and understands all the imaginations of your thoughts, what does He have in mind for you? Have you ever asked? Have you felt a prompting? *Be strong, and do it.* You might think you are not creative enough, or talented enough, or brave enough. But the Lord knows you are. He promises: "If thou seek him, he will be found of thee" (1 Chronicles 28:9). He will help you accomplish every great thing He has in mind for you. "Be strong and of good courage, and do it: fear not, nor be dismayed: for the Lord God . . . will not fail thee, nor forsake thee, until thou hast finished all the work for the service . . . of the Lord" (1 Chronicles 28:20). God believes in every one of us. —EBF

Reflect and Respond
What good thoughts fill your imagination right now?

Your favorite
scripture in
1 Kings 2

1 KINGS 3:5

Ask what I shall give thee.

Just after King David died, Solomon, his son, prepared to become king. The night before Solomon was to be made the king, the Lord appeared to him in a dream, saying, "Ask what I shall give thee" (1 Kings 3:5). Solomon was worried that he would not be equal to the task because he was young, he wasn't exactly sure what he was doing, and he was overwhelmed over the thought of how many people he would be serving. He asked, "Give . . . thy servant an understanding heart" (1 Kings 3:9). The Lord answered, "Because thou hast asked this thing, and hast not asked for thyself long life; neither hast asked riches for thyself . . . but hast asked for thyself understanding . . . Behold, I have done according to thy words . . . I have given thee a wise and an understanding heart" (1 Kings 3:11–12). I have come to respect Solomon for requesting this gift.

There is an interesting verse of scripture written many years after Solomon received this humble gift. In the book of Ecclesiastes, which some scholars have attributed to Solomon, we read, "And I gave my heart . . . yea, my heart had great experience" (Ecclesiastes 1:13, 16). I love the thought that in the beginning of his service Solomon asked for an understanding heart, and that many years later, perhaps it was he who wrote that his heart had great experience.

How do we learn to have an understanding heart? How do we give our hearts great experience?

One weekend when my children were young, I stayed at my mother's house. I was up all night, and so were my children, because of the barking of the neighbor's dog next door. One morning at breakfast I said to my mom, "You have got to do something about that dog."

"What dog?" my mom replied. I looked at her incredulously, "The dog next door; it was up barking all night last night, didn't you hear it?" My mom just kept eating her breakfast.

"I know that it is against the law to bark after 10:00 at night, so you could call the pound and they would send someone out," I told her. My mother just kept eating her breakfast. Finally, I said to her, "Does the dog not bother you?" "I don't hear the dog," my mom replied.

"How could you not *hear* the dog?" I asked, fearing that my mother was losing her hearing, or possibly her sanity, I wasn't sure which.

My mom explained that a few weeks before, the neighbor had called her. "I am calling to apologize for my dog," the neighbor said. "I know it must be a bother to you and your husband. But you need to know that I have a son, whom I adore, and he is going through a really hard time right now." She explained that the counselor they were working with had suggested they get a dog to see if that would give her son something to live for, and somehow it was working. "I am so sorry about the disturbance," she said, "but right now there is nothing else we can do." Then my mom looked across the table at me and said, "So when the dog starts barking, I don't hear the dog. What I hear is, '*I have a son, whom I adore,*' and the dog just doesn't bother me anymore."

It was a profound lesson. I had been so quick to judge. I knew what to do. We would call the pound and the matter would be resolved. My mother had taken a different route. She had an understanding heart, and it had allowed her heart to have great experience. Her willingness to love, rather than judge, made a huge difference in the relationship between her and her neighbor. To this day, even though they live miles apart, they are best friends. My mother's experience taught me to have an understanding heart, and this lesson has allowed my heart to have great experiences of its own. —EBF

Reflect and Respond

How could you be better at having an understanding heart?

Your favorite scripture in
1 Kings 3

1 KINGS 8:35

If they pray toward this place . . .

Solomon's dedicatory prayer upon the temple was filled with repetition consisting of two primary words: *if* and *then*.

"*If* they pray toward this place, and confess thy name, and turn from their sin . . . *then* hear thou in heaven, and forgive the sin of thy servants . . . that thou teach them the good way wherein they should walk" (1 Kings 8:35–36; emphasis added). "*If* there be in the land famine, if there be pestilence, . . . if their enemy besiege them . . . what prayer and supplication soever be made by any man . . . and spread forth his hands toward this house: *then* hear thou . . . and forgive, and do, and give to every man according to his ways" (1 Kings 8:37–39; emphasis added). "*If* they sin against thee, . . . yet if they shall bethink themselves . . . and repent, and make supplication unto thee . . . and so return unto thee with all their heart, and with all their soul . . . and pray unto thee toward . . . the house which I have built for thy name: *then* hear thou their prayer . . . and maintain their cause, . . . for they be thy people" (1 Kings 8:46–51; emphasis added).

Sometimes it is hard to accept the consequences of our actions. This was true for Solomon, the man with the wise and understanding heart whose first choice was to build a temple for his God. The consequence of this choice led to great blessings, but somewhere after this moment, Solomon began making choices that led to his fall. It might have been because he became fixated on foreign ideas. Perhaps his growing luxury became a weakness. We don't know Solomon's heart, but we do know this—Solomon's choices led him to a path that started with great happiness and ended with deep regret. In the end, he forgot the Lord. —EBF

Reflect and Respond

What have you learned about choices and consequences?

Your favorite scripture in 1 Kings 8

1 KINGS 12:7

**If thou wilt be a servant unto this people this day
. . . then they will be thy servants for ever**.

After the death of King Solomon, his son Rehoboam became the next king of Israel. One of the first things that happened during his reign was a meeting of all the people, who came to Rehoboam and begged him to lighten the heavy burdens that his father, Solomon, had placed upon them during his time as king. Rehoboam told the people he wanted time to think through what they had requested and to return in three days for an answer.

Rehoboam turned to the "old men" who served with his father (1 Kings 12:6) and consulted with them first. Their advice was to serve, answer, and speak good words to the people. They promised the king that if he did that, the people would be loyal to him forever. After hearing their advice, Rehoboam went to the young men—the friends he grew up with—and asked them what they thought. Their advice was opposite. They told Rehoboam to ignore the people and the old men and demand more of the people—to make their burdens heavier and promise more punishments. When the three days were up, the people of Israel came back together and heard Rehoboam's threats and unkind promises. It was bad enough that ten of the tribes revolted against Rehoboam and followed a new leader, Jeroboam. From this point in history, the united tribes were now split into two separate kingdoms—the northern kingdom of Israel, composed of ten of the twelve tribes, and the southern kingdom of Judah, made up of the tribes of Judah and Benjamin.

The advice the young men gave to Rehoboam was catastrophic to the nation. It was wise for him to seek the advice of the older men—those who had wisdom and could see things with a greater perspective. It would have been wiser had he taken their advice. —DB

Reflect and Respond

Who are your old men—the wise people you go to looking for advice? Why them?

Your favorite scripture in
1 Kings 12

1 KINGS 16:13

**By which they sinned,
and by which they made Israel to sin . . .**

Confucius, the great Chinese leader and philosopher, was reported to have said, "The character of a ruler is like wind and that of the people is like grass. In whatever direction the wind blows, the grass always bends." This was certainly true in ancient Israel. Through the books and chronicles of the kings, so much about the nations of Israel and Judah depended on their leaders. Generally speaking, if the nation was prospering, it was because the king was leading the people in righteousness and the people were following. There is so much we can learn from the righteous kings of Judah. We can learn equally powerful lessons from the unrighteous kings and queens of the northern kingdom, Israel.

One of the most infamous couples was Ahab and Jezebel. Ahab was already a wicked and idolatrous king before making a marriage alliance with Jezebel. When she came into Israel, she brought her perverted and immoral religious practices with her. Her strong influence had a devastating impact upon the people. The Bible Dictionary entry about Jezebel says that "this marriage, more than any other single event, caused the downfall of the northern kingdom." Together, she and Ahab "made Israel to sin."

Technically, no one can make another person sin, but the power of influence cannot be overstated. You might not have a king or queen like Ahab or Jezebel ruling over you, but each of us has chosen our own leaders of influence. Each of our hearts has a proverbial throne on it, and we decide who will rule and reign there. —DB

Reflect and Respond

Who are some of the most influential people in your life?
What are they making you to do?

Your favorite
scripture in
1 Kings 16

1 KINGS 17:16

**And the barrel of meal wasted not,
neither did the cruse of oil fail.**

When Elijah wandered into Zarephath, hungry and weary, the first person he met was an unnamed widow who the Lord said would sustain him. "Fetch me, I pray thee, a little water in a vessel, that I may drink," the tired prophet asked. As she turned to go, Elijah added one thing more to his request, "Bring me, I pray thee, a morsel of bread in thine hand" (1 Kings 17:10–11). Although the woman had known this prophet was coming, her circumstance was also dire. "I have not a cake," she replied, but only "an handful of meal in a barrel, and a little oil in a cruse" (1 Kings 17:12). It was to be the last meal she and her son would eat before they died. "Go," the prophet said, set aside your fear, "but make me thereof a little cake first, and bring it unto me, and after make for thee and for thy son" (1 Kings 17:13). I wonder what was in that mother's heart; perhaps there was a moment of pause as she considered the request. "Thus saith the Lord God of Israel," the weary prophet continued, "the barrel of meal shall not waste, neither shall the cruse of oil fail" (1 Kings 17:14). Not just for that meal on that day, the cruse and the barrel would sustain her for the rest of the famine in the land. "And she went and did" (1 Kings 17:15).

This thought of charity has filled my heart. Life has taught me that often the truest charity comes at the cost of greatest sacrifice. When I ponder the cruse of oil that will not fail in our time, I think of the men and women who have blessed my family's life with priesthood power and arms full of offerings. I think of charity that comes as we open our eyes to see suffering, even in times of our own distress, moments when we go and do, just as the widow of Zarephath did. —EBF

Reflect and Respond

How can you show charity today?

Your favorite
scripture in
1 Kings 17

1 KINGS 18:39

**And when all the people saw it, they fell on their
faces: and they said, The Lord, he is the God.**

After many years of hiding from the wicked king Ahab and queen Jezebel, Elijah
the prophet finally arranged a meeting with the king. He suggested a sort of showdown
on top of Mount Carmel so all the people could know once and for all who God truly
was and decide whether they would follow Him or not. Elijah invited the priests and
prophets of the false gods of Ahab and Jezebel to the mountaintop. There, they would
both build an altar of sacrifice and each call upon their own gods to send down fire from
heaven to consume the sacrifice.

The prophets of Baal began first. They built their altar and called upon their gods all
day long to answer with fire. But they didn't answer. Then it was Elijah's turn. He prepared an altar, laid on the sacrifice, and then in a surprising twist asked for four barrels
full of water to be poured over the altar. Then he asked for water to be poured again.
Once more, a third time, the water was poured, until the area was drenched in twelve
barrels of water. Then Elijah cried out to the Lord to send down fire. And flames came
flying out of heaven onto the altar, licking up the water, lighting the whole altar and
sacrifice in a fire so hot that everything was completely consumed. When the people saw
it, they fell to the ground in awe and proclaimed, "The Lord, he is the God." In that moment they knew. They knew the Lord God of Israel was a God of power.

We will also have Mount Carmel moments, times when the strength of heaven will
come down in miraculous ways and we will know that He is a God of power. Perhaps,
like the people on that mountaintop, we will also learn from time to time another powerful truth—that He would be a God of sacrifice, offering Himself completely. —DB

Reflect and Respond

*When have you had a fire from Carmel moment—a moment you
knew God was God?*

Your favorite
scripture in
1 Kings 18

1 KINGS 19:6

There was a cake baken on the coals, and a cruse of water.

There came a time when Jezebel declared Elijah as her enemy and sought to take his life. When Elijah found out, he ran. After a day's journey into the wilderness, he stopped to rest under a juniper tree. Surely he had been praying the entire journey, but here he breathed out a final prayer: "He requested for himself that he might die; . . . it is enough . . . O Lord," was the frightened prophet's plea, "take away my life" (1 Kings 19:4). Then he fell asleep.

While he slept, an angel came and baked a cake on a pile of coals and filled a cruse with water. Then the angel touched him, saying, "Arise and eat" (1 Kings 19:5). After he ate and drank, he lay down and slept again. A second time the angel came and touched him. "Arise and eat," the angel said, "because the journey is too great for thee" (1 Kings 19:7).

Think of a time when the journey has been too great for you, when giving up seemed easier than continuing on. Who was your angel? I want to be that angel, to learn to see the suffering, to watch for the signs of exhaustion, to show up in the giving up. I want to recognize those situations where the journey is too great, and I want to deliver a little cake with a glass of milk. Comfort food. Companionship. God-sent encouragement meant for giving courage.

"What doest thou here, Elijah?" the Lord asked when he was finally ready to start the journey again. "I, even I only, am left," he replied, "and they seek my life, to take it away" (1 Kings 19:13–14). His was too great a burden to carry alone. The Lord had an answer: "Elisha the son of Shaphat . . . shalt thou anoint to be prophet in thy room" (1 Kings 19:16). The Lord will send us both angels and companions to carry us through our greatest times of need. —EBF

Reflect and Respond

To whom could you deliver a little cake and a glass of milk today?

Your favorite scripture in 1 Kings 19

1 KINGS 22:8

There is yet one man . . . but I hate him.

Jehoshaphat, king of Judah, was a good man who strengthened himself against the ways and the doings of the world and walked in the way his father had taught him. Because of his righteousness, great blessings came to Jehoshaphat, "and he had riches and honour in abundance. And his heart was lifted up in the ways of the Lord" (2 Chronicles 17:5–6; see also vv. 12–13).

At one point, Jehoshaphat joined with Ahab, king of Israel, to fight Syria. This was not a wise decision, for King Ahab was a wicked man, a man who hated the Lord. But Jehoshaphat didn't ask the Lord, as had previously been his custom. Instead, he alone made the decision to join Ahab. Recognizing his mistake at the last minute, Jehoshaphat asked King Ahab to inquire of his prophets whether they should go to battle. Ahab's prophets gathered, but they did not listen to the Lord. They foretold victory. "But Jehoshaphat said, Is there not here a prophet of the Lord besides, that we might inquire of him? And the king of Israel said unto Jehoshaphat, There is yet one man, by whom we may inquire of the Lord: *but I hate him; for he never prophesied good unto me, but always evil*" (2 Chronicles 18:6–7; emphasis added).

Have you heard this sentiment before? Ahab didn't like what the prophet of the Lord had to say. It bothered him so much that he had grown to hate the prophet. However, likely because he knew he needed Jehoshaphat and his army, King Ahab called for Micaiah the prophet.

When the messenger went to get Micaiah, he said to him, "Behold, the words of the prophets declare good to the king with one assent; let thy word therefore, I pray thee, be like one of theirs, and speak thou good" (2 Chronicles 18:12). I am sure this messenger was looking out for Micaiah as he begged him to simply say exactly what everyone else was saying. But Micaiah said, "As the Lord liveth, even what my God saith, that will I speak" (2 Chronicles 18:13). When Micaiah arrived at the throne room, he prophesied that Ahab would die. Immediately Ahab turned to Jehoshaphat and said, "Did I not tell thee that he would not prophesy good unto me, but evil?" (2 Chronicles 18:17). Ahab was angry and ordered that Micaiah be put in prison and fed the bread and water of affliction until Ahab returned again in peace. Micaiah told him, "If thou certainly return in peace, then hath not the Lord spoken by me" (2 Chronicles 18:27).

So the two kings prepared for battle. Ahab must have been a little nervous, because he decided to disguise himself and told Jehoshaphat to wear the robes of a king. The Syrians wanted only to destroy Ahab, so when their captains saw Jehoshaphat dressed in royal robes, they surrounded him, thinking he was the king of Israel. "But Jehoshaphat cried out, and the Lord helped him; and God moved them to depart from him" (2 Chronicles 18:31). As the day went on, Ahab was wounded, and about the time the sun went down, he died.

When Jehoshaphat returned home, he spoke to one of his own trusted prophets. The prophet told him, "Shouldest thou help the ungodly, and love them that hate the Lord? therefore is wrath upon thee from before the Lord. Nevertheless there are good things found in thee, in that thou . . . hast prepared thine heart to seek God" (2 Chronicles 19:2–3).

Sometimes our choices are going to be wrong. Like Jehoshaphat, we might find ourselves in a situation we can't get out of on our own. The Lord will not force us to turn to Him; however, a day may come when we cry out for help. The Lord's response is certain every time. He will hear a Jehoshaphat. He knows the good to be found in each of us because He knows our hearts. In the disastrous battle, if we cry out to Him, He will be there. But He will also always send a prophet to keep us in the right way. —EBF

Reflect and Respond

What words of the prophet have been the greatest protection to you?

Your favorite scripture in 1 Kings 22

2 CHRONICLES 20:15

The battle is not yours, but God's.

There is one more lesson we learn from the great King Jehoshaphat. During his reign, a large multitude came against him. In this moment of dire need, he did what he had always done—he "set himself to seek the Lord" (2 Chronicles 20:3). Jehoshaphat proclaimed a fast throughout all the land, and then he stood in front of the house of the Lord and prayed to the Lord, reminding Him of His promise to "hear and help" in times of affliction: "O our God, . . . we have no might against this great company that cometh against us; *neither know we what to do: but our eyes are upon thee*" (2 Chronicles 20:9, 12; emphasis added).

How many times in our own lives have we faced that situation: *"I don't know what to do."* In these moments, when what is against us seems mightier than we are, how often is our first inclination to focus our eyes upon the Lord? King Jehoshaphat's first response was to petition the Lord in all of Israel's behalf. "And all Judah stood before the Lord, with their little ones, their wives, and their children. Then . . . came the Spirit of the Lord in the midst of the congregation; And he said, Hearken ye, all Judah, and ye inhabitants of Jerusalem, and thou king Jehoshaphat, Thus saith the Lord unto you, Be not afraid nor dismayed by reason of this great multitude; *for the battle is not yours, but God's*" (2 Chronicles 20:13–15; emphasis added).

Think of the greatest trial you face right now; consider your multitude of burdens. Have you set yourself to seek God? Our God is mightier than any multitude of burdens we could ever face. Only He can fight our battles, because only He knows what it will take to conquer them. We must never forget—the battle is not ours, but God's, and He is with us. —EBF

Reflect and Respond
How could you set yourself to seek the Lord first today?

Your favorite scripture in 2 Chronicles 20

2 KINGS 4:5

. . . and she poured out.

"What shall I do for thee?" (2 Kings 4:2). It was the prophet's immediate response to the certain woman who was crying in front of him. Her husband was dead; the creditor was coming to take her two sons. "What hast thou in the house?" Elisha asked (2 Kings 4:2). The woman was wanting for everything. The only thing that remained was one pot of oil.

"Go, borrow thee vessels abroad of all thy neighbours, even empty vessels; borrow not a few. And when thou are come in, thou shalt shut the door upon thee and upon thy sons, *and shalt pour out* into all those vessels, and thou shalt set aside that which is full" (2 Kings 4:3–4; emphasis added). So the boys brought her the vessels, and she poured out until every vessel was filled, and the oil never ran out. She paid her debt with some, and she and the boys lived on the rest.

Perhaps you are in a moment of great want. Maybe you feel you have been left empty as you consider how to best care for those you love. The Lord is capable of providing great miracles through the means we have, providing an increase from meager stores and empty reserves. He will enable us to pour out.

This has been true for me both spiritually and physically. There have been many evenings after caring for my family all day long when my reserves are empty, and I wonder if I have anything left to give. Without fail, the Lord has blessed my capacity, He has filled my reservoir, and I have been blessed to pour out to those I love. Through Him, I have never run out.

Sometimes, though, we have more abundant means. Another woman, described in 2 Kings 4:8 as a "great woman," exemplified using such means to bless others.

Every time the prophet Elisha visited the city Shunem, he would pass by the home of a woman who would offer him bread. One day this great woman said to her husband, "Behold now, I perceive that this is an holy man of God, which passeth by us continually" (2 Kings 4:9). Right away we learn two things about this woman. First, she knew that Elisha was a holy man, and second, we learn that he came to her house continually. One day the woman asked her husband if they could make a place for the prophet to stay—a little chamber with a bed, a table, a stool, and a candlestick.

It is important to note that what this woman offered did not require a lot of money, time, or great talent. She simply offered what she had. So the prophet Elisha came and stayed in this chamber. One day, out of gratitude, he called for the woman to come to him and he said, "Thou hast been careful for us with all this care; what is to be done for thee?" (2 Kings 4:13). He wondered if he should say good things about her to the king or the captain of the host. But the woman answered, "I dwell among mine own people" (2 Kings 4:13). In other words, *I am happy just the way things are, and I don't expect anything in return for my service.* This woman was happy to serve without a reward.

I find it fitting that her quiet act of kindness remains secret today. We know her story, but we are never told her name. Think about the people within your circle of influence, those who walk past you every day. Is there something you could offer them? Can you think of a way you might serve them? Has the Lord blessed you with something that would allow you to touch their lives for good? Did you notice this great woman was not asked to serve? She wasn't given an assignment. Her actions for good were not extended because of a calling she held.

She simply saw a need and she filled it.

That is the mark of a great woman. —EBF

Reflect and Respond

How could you see a need and "pour out" to fill it today?

Your favorite scripture in 2 Kings 4

2 KINGS 5:13

**If the prophet had bid thee do some great thing,
wouldest thou not have done it?**

Naaman was a successful captain of the armies of the king of Syria—a neighboring country to Israel. He was a powerful ruler over many things and considered a great, courageous, and honorable man. He was also a leper. Even though he had legions at his command, he was powerless against this disease. Nothing in Syria could help him. Fortunately for him, there was a little maid in his household who had been taken captive from Israel. This girl knew of the prophet of the Lord who lived in her homelands who could help Naaman find the healing power of God. At her encouragement, Naaman went to Israel.

When Naaman arrived, Elisha did not even come out to meet him, but rather sent him to the Jordan River to wash seven times. Naaman was irritated that the prophet did no great thing for him, but instead asked him to do something so simple and seemingly meaningless. Frustrated, Naaman began his journey back home. Fortunately, Naaman had yet another servant who encouraged him to listen to the prophet's words and cleanse himself in the river.

And so he did. And after his seventh dip, Naaman came out of the water clean. He also came out of the river a believer. Before he returned home, Naaman asked for two loads of dirt to take with him. Perhaps the simplicity of the dirt would serve as a reminder to Naaman that a single, simple moment with God was more powerful than years of his overwhelming disease, and that he could take the holiness and goodness of God with him wherever he lived or went. Because He would always be only one simple step away. —DB

Reflect and Respond

In what ways have you found the power and presence of God through simple means?

Your favorite
scripture in
2 Kings 5

2 KINGS 6:16

They that be with us are more than they that be with them.

In this chapter we are told that the king of Syria warred against Israel. My imagination contrives a constant battle. Ongoing. Tiring. I have known times like that, when it seems someone has a constant agenda to fight against all that I am trying to accomplish. In this case, the prophet was on Israel's side. True to his calling, he sent direction and warning. The king of Israel followed this prophet's advice, and his life was spared "not once nor twice" (2 Kings 6:10). We are led to believe that his life was spared every time he followed the counsel of the prophet.

It didn't take long before the king of Syria became frustrated. He wondered if there was a spy in his camp. One of his servants pointed out that Elisha was the one getting in the way of his plan to destroy Israel. So he decided to capture Elisha. When he found out Elisha was in Dothan, the king sent "horses, and chariots, and a great host: and they came by night, and compassed the city about" (2 Kings 6:14).

I can imagine the servant of the prophet rising early that next morning. I picture him preparing for the journey ahead, gathering supplies for the trek to Samaria. I can understand the worry that must have filled his heart after seeing that the city was encompassed round about. I can almost hear the fear in his voice as he approaches Elisha, "Alas, my master! how shall we do?" (2 Kings 6:15). It feels real to me because I have felt that worry, that sense of imminent defeat, the fear that I am not enough to face the task in front of me. There have been times when my purpose seems to be threatened by what appears to be an enemy much stronger and more organized than I am. In this crucial moment, Elisha replied with confidence, "Fear not: for they that be with us are more than they that be with them" (2 Kings 6:16). Then he prayed and asked the Lord to "open his eyes, that he may see" (2 Kings 6:17). The Lord opened the eyes of the servant, and he beheld that the mountain was full of horses and chariots of fire. Heaven's help.

In this story, we are taught a principle that we must never forget. The unseen presence of God and of His help is real. If our eyes could be opened to see, we would realize that we do not ever wage a battle for righteousness alone. The Lord is with us. Heavenly help attends us. This knowledge alone should give us all the encouragement we need to move forward.

But there is a second lesson in the story: with the help of the Lord, Elisha and his servant were able to make it safely to Samaria, leading the Syrian army captive behind them. Safely protected by the Lord, they accomplished an unbelievable feat without weapons, without even the help of an army—simply with heaven's help. I love the condition of Elisha's heart at the end of this remarkable journey. The king of Israel asked Elisha when he saw him, "Shall I smite them? shall I smite them? And he answered, Thou shalt not smite them . . . set bread and water before them, that they may eat and drink, and go to their master" (2 Kings 6:21–22).

I often wonder if my heart is in the same place, because it seems like perhaps I would not be so kind to those who have tried to frustrate my purpose. My first inclination seems to lean more toward revenge or retribution than to hospitality or compassion. Perhaps it is heaven's help that I must turn to in these moments also. Maybe, once again, I need to pray to the Lord that He might open my eyes to see.

We must learn to trust the unseen, to rely on the certain presence of God's help even when our mortal eyes can't comprehend it, to believe that they that be with us are greater than they that be with them. The Lord can open our eyes to see both angel armies and also a way for compassion. Then we too can be part of the *greater* host: the Lord's army. —EBF

Reflect and Respond

When have your eyes been opened to see heaven's help?

Your favorite scripture in 2 Kings 6

2 KINGS 19:20

That which thou hast prayed . . . I have heard.

Hezekiah's story is one of my favorite stories in the entire Bible. It brings me comfort. It testifies of prayer. It speaks of hope. To fully understand the magnitude of Hezekiah's experience, we first have to come to know Hezekiah. The scriptures teach us that he did that which was right in the sight of the Lord. He trusted in the Lord God of Israel. He clave to the Lord and departed not from following Him. He kept His commandments. And the Lord was with him (see 2 Kings 18).

On one occasion, it seemed that all was conspiring against Hezekiah. I am intrigued by two questions that were asked of him by those who didn't share his beliefs: "What confidence is this wherein thou trustest? . . . Now on whom dost thou trust?" (2 Kings 18:19–20). Eventually those questions led Hezekiah to receive a letter filled with threats and deceit. Hezekiah went up into the house of the Lord and spread the letter before the Lord. And he prayed. He asked the Lord for a blessing, that his people would be saved, "that all the kingdoms of the earth may know that thou art the Lord God, even thou only" (2 Kings 19:19).

The Lord's prophet, Isaiah, sent to Hezekiah, saying, "Thus saith the Lord God of Israel, That which thou hast prayed . . . I have heard" (2 Kings 19:20). I believe this experience and conversation with the Lord prepared Hezekiah's heart for a future trial.

The scriptures tell us, "In those days was Hezekiah sick unto death" (2 Kings 20:1). The chapter explains that he had a wound, one that wouldn't heal. Isaiah came to Hezekiah and told him that he needed to set his house in order, for he was going to die. Hezekiah turned his face to the wall and wept sore. And he prayed: "I beseech thee, O Lord, remember now how I have walked before thee in truth and with a perfect heart, and have done that which is good in thy sight" (2 Kings 20:3). Before Isaiah had even left the middle court, the voice of the Lord came to him, saying, "Turn again, and tell Hezekiah . . . Thus saith the Lord . . . I have heard thy prayer, I have seen thy tears:

behold, I will heal thee. . . . And I will add unto thy days . . . and I will deliver thee . . . and I will defend this city" (2 Kings 20:5–6; emphasis added).

My thoughts turn to healing, and to the power of prayer, because I have experienced the darkest moments of life. The moments that cause you to turn your face to the wall. The moments that invoke you to weep sore. Sometimes those moments come even after we have walked in truth, with a perfect heart, even when we are doing that which is good. In those moments, we, like Hezekiah, are in need of healing. Often the wound is so deep, it requires the kind of healing that can only come from the Lord. "O Lord, remember . . ." Remember me. The story of Hezekiah teaches that we are not forgotten of the Lord. Even when the trials of life seem to destroy us, especially at times when others might ask, "What confidence is this wherein thou trustest? Now on whom dost thou trust?" In those moments, weeping sore, we must turn to the Lord. We must pray.

Life has taught me that healing comes in many ways. Sometimes healing means saving a life or healing an illness. But sometimes the illness lingers. Sometimes the life isn't saved. Even then—*especially* then—healing is required, a healing of the heart. A wounded heart can cause us to turn our face to the wall, to weep sore, but hopefully, it will also lead us to call on the Lord through prayer. Because the healing of life's deepest wounds can only come through Him. It is that kind of healing that causes us to testify, I know "that thou art the Lord God, *even thou only*" (2 Kings 19:19; emphasis added). —EBF

Reflect and Respond
When has the Lord heard and answered your prayer?

Your favorite scripture in 2 Kings 19

2 CHRONICLES 30:1

Come to the house of the Lord.

The first thing Hezekiah did when he began to reign was to open the doors of the temple. There is significance in this moment, for it was in his heart "to make a covenant with the Lord God of Israel" (2 Chronicles 29:10). But Hezekiah was not satisfied with just making a change in his own life. His capacity to love and to lead was magnified, and he extended that invitation to change to everyone within his reach. He "sent to all Israel and Judah, and wrote letters also to Ephraim and Manasseh, that they should come to the house of the Lord at Jerusalem" (2 Chronicles 30:1). Some laughed him to scorn and mocked him. Nevertheless, some humbled themselves and came. "And they stood in their place" (2 Chronicles 30:16). Because of a simple invitation, extended by a humble man, a very great congregation gathered. "And Hezekiah rejoiced, and all the people, that God had prepared the people: *for the thing was done suddenly*" (2 Chronicles 29:36; emphasis added).

This story reminds me of the great power that one righteous person can have. It testifies of the power of one in changing the lives of many. I love that it can happen suddenly. What can we learn about leadership from the story of Hezekiah? The scriptures tell us he had a gift for speaking to the heart. Encouragingly. Intimately. He prayed for his people, asking the Lord to pardon everyone and to heal them. He "wrought that which was good and right and truth before the Lord his God" (2 Chronicles 31:20). But my favorite characteristic of all is found in verse 21 of chapter 31, "In every work that he began . . . he did it with all his heart." —EBF

Reflect and Respond

What endeavor have you taken with your whole heart?

Your favorite scripture in
2 Chronicles 30

2 CHRONICLES 31:10

The Lord hath blessed his people; and that which is left is this great store.

Hezekiah was a king the people gathered to and listened to. "And the people rested themselves [or relied] upon the words of Hezekiah king of Judah" (2 Chronicles 32:8). The Lord fought their battles and guided them on every side and blessed them. Through Hezekiah's leadership, the people learned to be encouraged in the laws of the Lord. This allowed great blessings to come to the people.

It is in Hezekiah's story that we first read about the principle of tithing. As the people paid their tithes, they laid them in heaps. In the third month they began to lay the foundation of the heaps, the storehouses, and they finished them in the seventh month. Then Hezekiah came to see the heaps, and when he saw them, he blessed the Lord and His people Israel. Then he questioned why there was so much abundance in the heaps. I love the answer Hezekiah was given by Azariah, the chief priest. "Since the people began to bring the offerings into the house of the Lord, we have had enough to eat, and have left plenty: for the Lord hath blessed his people; and that which is left is this great store" (2 Chronicles 31:10). I think of these heaps, these storehouses, filled with the blessings poured out from the Lord.

When I read this story, I can't help but be reminded of a scripture found in Malachi, "Bring ye all the tithes into the storehouse . . . and prove me now herewith, saith the Lord of hosts, if I will not open you the *windows of heaven,* and pour you out a blessing, that there shall not be room enough to receive it" (Malachi 3:10; emphasis added). Right there in 2 Chronicles we find a tangible second witness of the promise penned in Malachi: heaps of blessings. —EBF

Reflect and Respond

How have you experienced the blessings from paying tithing?

Your favorite scripture in 2 Chronicles 31

2 KINGS 22:2

. . . and turned not aside to the right hand or to the left.

It doesn't take long when reading the book of Kings to realize that the wicked kings far outnumber the righteous ones. The description of the wicked kings is often marked with a similar phrase: one king "walked in all the sins of his father" (1 Kings 15:3), another "did evil in the sight of the Lord, and walked in the way of his father [Jeroboam]" (1 Kings 15:26), a third "walked in the way of the kings of Israel" (2 Chronicles 21:6), and still another "walked in the ways of the house of Ahab" (2 Chronicles 22:3). However, there is one king who is described differently. Josiah "did that which was right in the sight of the Lord, and walked in all the way of David his father, and turned not aside to the right hand or to the left" (2 Kings 22:2).

This idea of walking without turning aside to the right hand or the left, of walking in righteousness, is intriguing because the percentage of kings who walked in righteousness during their reign is so small. I want to celebrate their dedication. I want to learn from their diligence. I want to live my life without turning aside to the right hand or the left.

Mary Fielding Smith, an early pioneer, once described herself as "having not the smallest desire to go one step backward."[18] From the book of Kings, we can understand the importance of that desire. Perhaps we could be more like that. Maybe we could consider what it means to turn neither to the right hand or the left, to do what is right in the sight of the Lord, and may we have not the smallest desire to go one step backward. —EBF

Reflect and Respond

What gives you the courage and determination to turn neither to the right hand or the left?

Your favorite scripture in 2 Kings 22

2 KINGS 23:3

**The king . . . made a covenant before the Lord . . . to
perform the words . . . that were written in this book.**

The end of Chronicles echoes of the end of Kings. The authority passing from father to son. The never knowing if the king would reign in righteousness or in wickedness. Each generation choosing. Once more we read of Josiah. During the reign of Josiah, a sacred book was found in the house of the Lord. Josiah asked those who had the book, "Go, inquire of the Lord for me . . . concerning the words of the book" (2 Chronicles 34:21).

Then Josiah, the king whose heart was tender, sent and gathered together all the elders, "and all the men of Judah, and the inhabitants of Jerusalem, and the priests, and the Levites, and all the people, *great and small:* and he read in their ears all the words of the book of the covenant that was found in the house of the Lord.

"And the king stood in his place, and made a covenant before the Lord, to walk after the Lord, and to keep his commandments, and his testimonies, and his statutes, with all his heart, and with all his soul, to perform the words of the covenant which are written in this book. And he caused all that were present in Jerusalem . . . to stand to it. And the inhabitants of Jerusalem did" (2 Chronicles 34:30–32; emphasis added).

"And he . . . encouraged them to the service of the house of the Lord, and said . . . prepare yourselves . . . and stand in the holy place" (2 Chronicles 35:2–5).

Josiah teaches us the power of gathering together to read the words of God and the strength that lies therein. We must stand in that place and learn more of the covenants—we must learn to walk, to keep the commandments and the testimonies and the statutes with all our hearts, with all our souls. To stand to it. To act upon what we learn.

When our home was being built, we would stop by every evening to watch the progress. One evening, just after the footings had been laid but before the cement floor had been poured, we gathered together as a family to talk about what it means to lay a foundation. We were all there, *the great and the small.* We told our children, *If the foundation is firm, it will provide a base for something to stand on. A home.* We wanted to remember that a firm foundation would allow us to stand for what we believed in, and we talked about what would make our foundation firm.

Scriptures
Testimony
And Prayer
Night and
Day
STAND.

When we were finished talking, we each took off one of our shoes, and we buried them in the ground next to one of the footings. The next day they poured cement over the hole. The shoes remain buried next to our foundation today as a testimony of our covenant—a reminder of the important decision we made as a family to keep the words of the Lord in our life, to prepare ourselves to stand in a holy place. —EBF

Reflect and Respond

What covenants have you made because of the words of the book?

Your favorite scripture in 2 Kings 23

2 KINGS 25:2

**And the city was besieged unto the
eleventh year of king Zedekiah.**

The Lord sent prophet after prophet to warn the city of Jerusalem of their dangerous neighbor Babylon. He could protect them, as He had in the past, if they would just allow Him to. Instead, the people of Judah turned their backs on their Lord, just as the northern kingdom had. And, just like the northern kingdom of Israel, the southern kingdom of Judah was attacked and run over by an enemy nation. 2 Kings 25 is the account of Nebuchadnezzar's siege on the city of Jerusalem.

The description is awful. Not only were the people dealing with a long-term famine, but Nebuchadnezzar came in with even more fury and vengeance. The Babylonian army broke through all the walls of the city. The king, Zedekiah, watched his sons killed in front of him before his eyes were taken out and he was carried away as a slave in chains. Nebuchadnezzar's army burnt the temple and all the great houses of Jerusalem to the ground. There was a great massacre among the people, and the majority of the survivors were taken away into captivity.

One of the prophets sent to warn the people of Jerusalem about an avoidable destruction was Lehi. In the beginning of the Book of Mormon, we discover that he both warned the city and then left with his family during the reign of King Zedekiah. Out in the wilderness, his own sons complained against him and said, "These many years we have suffered . . . which time we might have enjoyed our possessions . . . yea, and we might have been happy" (1 Nephi 17:21). The 2 Kings 25 account proves otherwise. I don't think they would have been happy had they stayed. The Lord protected and preserved them through the warning of their father prophet. —DB

Reflect and Respond

*What protection and preservation have you noticed by listening to
the Lord's warning voice?*

Your favorite
scripture in
2 Kings 25

EZRA 1:1

That the word of the Lord by the mouth of Jeremiah might be fulfilled, the Lord stirred up the spirit of Cyrus.

Even though the children of Israel were in captivity and exile in Babylon for more than seventy years, they held on to the promises the Lord made through His prophets that they would one day return to the city of Jerusalem and rebuild it. The time of Ezra and Nehemiah was the era when those prophecies began to be fulfilled.

The empire of Persia conquered Babylon, the nation that was holding the Israelites captive. In the first year of the Persian king Cyrus, the Lord stirred up the spirit of Cyrus, and he issued a decree for a group of the children of Israel to return to Jerusalem to begin to rebuild. The first group was led by a man named Zerubbabel, who had the call and mission to rebuild the temple. He went with the resources and blessings of the king of Persia to do this most important work.

Sometime later, another king of Persia, Artaxerxes, was stirred up in a similar way to send Ezra, "a ready scribe" who had "prepared his heart to seek the law of the Lord, and to do it" (Ezra 7:6, 10) to lead another group of people back to Jerusalem to teach the people the word of the Lord and establish their rituals, their learning, and their faith community again. Both of these great men and others went and rebuilt and made Jerusalem a beautiful city again.

I love thinking of Ezra as a ready scribe. Before his moment came, he was preparing himself and his heart to do the work God would call him to do. Perhaps you are being stirred up by the Spirit right now to do a work, or perhaps you are in a place of preparing for a future day when that call will come. —DB

Reflect and Respond

What are you doing now to prepare your heart for when it is stirred up to do good?

Your favorite scripture in
Ezra 1

NEHEMIAH 3:12

Shallum the son of Halohesh, the ruler of the half part
of Jerusalem, **he and his daughters.**

Nehemiah was the king's cupbearer. This one detail found in the last verse of the first chapter of his book is important: it lets us know that Nehemiah was a man of great courage because it was his job to make sure the king's cup had not been poisoned. Nehemiah's humble prayer found in chapter one touches my heart. The walls of Jerusalem had been destroyed, and Nehemiah wanted permission to rebuild the city. He prayed for walls to be repaired and gates to be mended; the burden of it consumed his countenance. When the king saw him sad, he asked why. Nehemiah replied, "Why should not my countenance be sad, when the city, the place of my fathers' sepulchres, lieth waste, and the gates thereof are consumed with fire?" (Nehemiah 2:3). The king asked him, "For what dost thou make request?" Nehemiah's answer consisted of five simple words, "that I may build it" (Nehemiah 2:4–5).

He arose in the night and viewed the wall. He saw the destruction. He understood the work that would be required. Then he gathered the people together, saying, "See the distress that we are in . . . come, and let us build up the wall of Jerusalem" (Nehemiah 2:17). Impressed by Nehemiah's great desire, the people gathered together and prepared to work. Meanwhile, the enemies of Jerusalem gathered together in opposition. They pointed fingers at the people, they despised them, and as they laughed, they said, "What is this thing that ye do?" (Nehemiah 2:19). And Nehemiah answered, "The God of heaven, he will prosper us; therefore we his servants will arise and build" (Nehemiah 2:20).

Chapter three is a list of the builders of the wall. We read of the high priests, the men of Jericho, sons and fathers, the men of Gibeon, and the goldsmiths. And then, in verse twelve, we read of "Shallum the son of Halohesh, the ruler of the half part of Jerusalem, he and his daughters."

I love that the daughters are mentioned. These were girls intent on building up the kingdom, daughters who were willing to work alongside the high priests and the goldsmiths and the fathers and the sons. The daughters of Shallum. They showed up to build.

Let us remember this, those of us who are daughters in this church. There is nothing that should hold us back from building the Lord's kingdom. There are walls to repair and gates to be mended. We don't need a title. We don't need a talent. We just need to show up. —EBF

Reflect and Respond

What do you learn from this story about showing up?

Your favorite scripture in
Nehemiah 3

NEHEMIAH 6:3

I am doing a great work, so that I cannot come down: why should the work cease . . . ?

Previously we read that Artaxerxes, the Persian king, sent Nehemiah and a group of people back to Jerusalem to work on rebuilding the walls of the city. It didn't take long for the enemies of the Jews to catch wind of the project, which they quickly mocked! But Nehemiah and his crew ignored their insults and continued their work. To the surprise of these enemies, the work continued and actually began to progress quickly. They mounted their forces to come to the wall and physically stop Nehemiah and his people from finishing the job.

One particular enemy, Sanballat, sent a letter to Nehemiah to come meet him in a nearby valley. Nehemiah, knowing that Sanballat's intentions were wicked and that he was trying to distract him, answered, "I am doing a great work, so that I cannot come down." Sanballat made three more attempts to get Nehemiah to leave the wall and come meet with him, and Nehemiah answered the same each time. *This work is too great, I cannot come down.*

We still have enemies who mock us and distract us from the work that God has called us to do—people who will tempt us to live on a lower level. Avoiding these temptations and quickly saying no is good advice, but maybe, like Nehemiah, instead of saying no to our "Sanballats," we can say yes to God. If we allow our hearts to be captured by the greatness and wonder of the work of the Lord, we will be better able to stay focused and finish what He has called us to do. —DB

Reflect and Respond

What is the great work that your heart and efforts are focused on right now?

Your favorite scripture in Nehemiah 6

NEHEMIAH 8:18

Day by day, from the first day unto the last day . . .

Ezra was a powerful teacher in the Old Testament. "Ezra had *prepared his heart* to seek the law of the Lord, and *to do it,* and to *teach*" (Ezra 7:10; emphasis added). We can learn from him: if we want to be powerful witnesses for the Lord, we must *prepare our hearts* to understand His words, then we must *act on what we learn,* and we must *teach* what we know to others.

Because Ezra possessed the wisdom of God, he was asked to teach all those who did not already know the laws of God. "And he read therein before the street that was before the water gate from the morning until midday, before the men and the women, and those that could understand; and the ears of all the people were attentive unto the book of the law" (Nehemiah 8:3). As Ezra read, he "gave the sense," or in other words, expanded the meaning and caused them to understand (Nehemiah 8:8). For seven days Ezra taught, "day by day, from the first day unto the last day" (Nehemiah 8:18). We learn that the people were attentive, they wept and prayed as they listened to the words, they understood what they were learning, and there was a very great gladness (see Nehemiah 8:3, 6, 9, 12, 17).

What do you learn from the descriptions above? Why was Ezra such a good teacher? Think for a minute about the opportunities you have to teach. You might be a teacher in your own home, your profession, or your Church calling. Opportunities to teach happen every single day. Are we learning to love the scriptures like Ezra did? Are we preparing our hearts *to do* what we are learning? Even more important, are we teaching what we are learning? We should. From morning until midday. Day by day. From the first day unto the last day. —EBF

Reflect and Respond

What lesson from Ezra could you apply to your teaching?

Your favorite scripture in Nehemiah 8

NEHEMIAH 12:8

. . . and Mattaniah, which was over the thanksgiving . . .

Have you ever noticed the priest named Mattaniah in the Old Testament, who, with his brethren, was over the thanksgiving? I am fascinated by him. I decided for my next job I want to be the person over the thanksgiving. Imagine what would fill your thoughts if you were constantly in charge of giving thanks. What if it was your job "to praise and to give thanks" all day, every single day? (Nehemiah 12:24).

I love the image of the people that Nehemiah sent up upon the wall on the day of dedication to give thanks: "Then I brought up the princes of Judah upon the wall, and appointed two great companies of them that gave thanks" (Nehemiah 12:31). I can picture Ezra leading one company with musical instruments down the one side of the wall, the other company walking down the other side of the wall with Nehemiah following behind. I would have loved to have been there on that day to witness the thanksgiving, the rejoicing, the great joy, so great that it was heard even afar off. "Also that day they offered great sacrifices, and rejoiced: for *God had made them rejoice with great joy:* the wives also and the children rejoiced: so that the joy of Jerusalem was heard even afar off" (Nehemiah 12:43; emphasis added).

Perhaps today could be a day like that, filled with rejoicing and great joy and thanksgiving. What if you put yourself in charge of the thanksgiving? Starting from sunup, what if you filled your thoughts with gratitude?

Already my thoughts are filling with thanksgiving. And I wonder, how full will my thoughts be with the setting of the sun? How full of gratitude? How full of joy? —EBF

Reflect and Respond
How could you be in charge of the thanksgiving today?

Your favorite scripture in **Nehemiah 12**

ESTHER 4:14

**Who knoweth whether thou art come to the
kingdom for such a time as this?**

In the book of Esther we read of an evil man named Haman who wanted all of the Jews to be put to death. Queen Esther was afraid for her uncle Mordecai and all of her people. She didn't know what to do, so she sent one of her servants to ask Mordecai's advice. Mordecai told Queen Esther to go to the king and tell him that she was a Jew and ask him to save her people, who had done nothing wrong to the king.

But Esther was scared. There was a rule in the kingdom, punishable by death, that no one could go in to speak to the king unless they were called for by name, and Esther had not been called in to see the king. She reminded Mordecai of the grave danger she would be in if she chose to approach the king uninvited.

Now, here comes my favorite part of the story: The servant returned to Esther with Mordecai's answer. Mordecai knew how dangerous it would be for Esther to stand up for her people. He had raised Esther as his daughter, and he loved her. I imagine he must have been so worried about Esther. But still, he gave her great counsel. He reaffirmed the importance of her mission to save her people and then said, "Who knoweth whether thou art come to the kingdom for such a time as this?" (Esther 4:14). In other words, you have been sent here to earth with a specific mission to fulfill, and the events of your life have been orchestrated such that you are in the right place at the right time, and this is your moment to shine.

Now, that may have been true, but it didn't make it less scary.

Queen Esther thought long and hard about what she was about to do. Finally, she sent her servant back to Mordecai with her answer, "Go, gather together all the Jews . . . and fast ye for me, and neither eat nor drink three days, night or day: I also and my maidens will fast likewise; and so will I go in unto the king, which is not according to the law: and if I perish, I perish" (Esther 4:16).

Queen Esther decided to stand up for what she believed. She chose to fulfill her divine mission, knowing that it might mean she would die. In this moment it is important to notice one essential detail: *She did not go in to the king alone.* Mordecai and all of the Jews were fasting for her. And she and all of her best friends were fasting. Queen Esther approached the king knowing that the strength of her people, her friends, and, most importantly, the Lord, was with her.

And so, on the third day, even though the king had not called her name, Esther put on her fancy clothing and stood in the inner court of the king's house. And the king sat upon his royal throne.

When the king saw Esther, the queen, standing all dressed up in the middle of the court, he remembered how much he loved her, and he raised his golden scepter. Then Esther came to him and touched the top of the scepter, and she was allowed to speak without being put to death.

The king said, "What wilt thou, queen Esther? and what is thy request?" (Esther 5:3). Queen Esther invited the king to a banquet, where she reminded him of the evil decree and told him she was a Jew, and then she begged him to save her life, and the lives of her people. The king wondered how such an awful thing could happen, and Esther told the king that his servant was a wicked man, and his enemy.

So, Haman, the evil man, was put to death.

And Esther and her people were saved. —EBF

Reflect and Respond

Why were you sent to this kingdom in such a time as this?

Your favorite scripture in Esther 1–4

ESTHER 9:19

A day of gladness . . . and a good day . . .

In the book of Esther, we learn that after everything had finally calmed down, the Jews celebrated. Their enemies had been slain, Haman and his ten sons had been killed, and throughout the land, the Jews gathered to rejoice in their deliverance and victory. I love the description of this event found in Esther 9:19, "a day of gladness . . . and a good day." Have you ever had one of those days? A day of gladness and a good day.

Take a second to think about some of your best days. Were they days of gladness? Looking back, would you list them as good days?

Have you ever noticed that what makes some of the best days is when we choose to remember the good part of that day? If we want to experience days of gladness and good days, we must choose to focus on the good parts of those days. The scriptures teach this. It is spoken of in Luke, in a scripture that is familiar to all of us, "and Mary hath chosen that good part" (Luke 10:42). It is referenced again when Lehi, who is at the end of his life, says, "I have spoken these few words unto you all, my sons, in the last days of my probation; and I have chosen the good part" (2 Nephi 2:30). The good part was something they *chose*. I believe that we too can choose the good part every single day. The choice is a powerful one and can change our lives—*for good*.

Perhaps at the end of each day, you could go over the moments and memories you have experienced, and you could choose to remember the good parts. As you gather those memories, maybe you could take a moment to rejoice in them. Then your life will be full to overflowing with days of gladness and good days. —EBF

Reflect and Respond

When was your last day of gladness? What made it a good day?

Your favorite scripture in Esther 9

JOB 42:2-3

I know that thou canst do every thing . . .
things too wonderful for me.

The book of Job scares me sometimes. Reading Job's story brings out the realist in me and reminds me how fragile life can be. Have you ever faced times when you have nothing left to give? Have the circumstances of life ever taken so much from you that it feels as if your whole soul has been carved out? Who fills the empty places?

It was in the still moments of Job's life that the answer to this question became clear.

"Hearken unto this, O Job: stand still, and consider the wondrous works of God" (Job 37:14). We must remember, God knew from the very beginning what was about to happen to Job. He knew about the trials, but He also knew about the blessings. More important, He knew about the learning, and what it would take to make Job's life experience complete. He knew how to fill the empty places in Job's soul. "I know that thou canst do every thing . . . things too wonderful for me, which I knew not" (Job 42:2–3).

Although his life was filled with disappointment and discouragement, Job was blessed abundantly. At the end of his life, every empty place was filled. "The Lord gave Job twice as much as he had before . . . so the Lord blessed the latter end of Job more than his beginning" (Job 42:10, 12). Elder Joseph B. Wirthlin explains, "The Lord compensates the faithful for every loss. That which is taken away from those who love the Lord will be added unto them in His own way. While it may not come at the time we desire, the faithful will know that every tear today will eventually be returned a hundredfold with tears of rejoicing and gratitude."[19] —EBF

Reflect and Respond

How has the Lord filled the empty places in your soul?

Your favorite scripture in
Job 42

PSALM 1:3

**And he shall be like a tree planted by the rivers of water,
that bringeth forth his fruit in his season.**

The first of the Psalms seems to be all about finding happiness. When you look around you, or within you, you may notice that there are times of great happiness, times of discontent, and everything in between. What is it that leads us to that blessed, happy state? What is the secret? It doesn't seem to come naturally, but instead is a result of something deliberate.

The Psalmist first advises us how *not* to find it. Sitting or resting in ungodliness, sin, and scorning are not the way to what we are looking for. Instead, the Psalmist compares us to a tree and teaches that where or what we are planted in makes all the difference. Blessed is the man whose "delight is in the law of the Lord; and in his law doth he meditate day and night" (Psalm 1:2). The laws of the Lord are not a list of His rules but a guide to His central message of covenant love and devotion to Israel. And happy will be the man or woman who delights in that love (or is planted in it) and meditates on it night and day.

In the first Psalm, that tree is planted next to rivers of water that represent that covenant love of God. I imagine the roots of that tree, right by the water's edge, drinking deeply of that love. And even though the tree will not always have fruit—there will always be seasons of plenty and seasons of none—the leaves will never wither. The tree will always be alive on the inside, despite what is happening on the outside. Inner contentment and happiness come from being planted in God's love. —DB

Reflect and Respond

What are you doing to plant yourself in the love of the Lord?

Your favorite scripture in **Psalm 1**

PSALM 5:3

**In the morning will I direct my prayer
unto thee, and will look up.**

The morning began with a prayer: gratitude, asking, pleading. Before the routine of the day began to flurry all around me, I directed my prayer unto Him. It was then that I remembered the last two words of counsel I had read in my scriptures the night before: *look up.*

"What does that mean?" I wondered as I raced up the stairs to quickly edit Meg's paper before her ride came. I pondered it again as I drove Grace to school in the early dawn hours before the sun peeked over the mountain. It was on my mind as I went for a walk around my neighborhood. Still there as I rotated the laundry, folded warm clothes, and hung them in the closet.

"What is that verse trying to teach?" I pondered it still as I read through the letters from two missionary sons. Thought about it as I wrote grocery lists for two different stores. Considered it as I grabbed my phone, and my keys, and my list of things to do. It was as I was driving home from the grocery store that the prompting finally came: *why don't you try it?*

Look up.

I really wanted to learn the lesson, so I pulled the car over right that second and parked. I stopped looking at the course ahead of me, the list down in my lap, the phone sitting next to me. I opened the car door, stepped out, and looked up. In that instant my focus changed, and my perspective became guided by God. I have learned the lesson. I am spending far too much time looking ahead, looking down, looking aimlessly. It is not often enough that I find myself looking up. —EBF

Reflect and Respond

Try looking up today. What do you discover?

Your favorite scripture in
Psalm 5

PSALM 17:5

Hold up my goings in thy paths,
that my footsteps slip not.

One summer morning we went for a hike. We walked up a riverbed—under trees, over rocks, cool water spilling over sandaled feet. It was one of those rare hikes you wish would just keep going and going. But it wasn't long before we rounded a bend and saw a waterfall with a sheer rock wall rising on either side. For just a moment we thought we had reached the end of the hike. Eyes wandered longingly to the scenery that beckoned to us from up above the waterfall.

And then, just there to the right, we saw the footholds that had been carved into the rock wall. Even now, as I think about it, my heart sinks right into my feet. There was a rope anchored above, but also a dropoff below. You could see where the footholds ended at the top, but I couldn't see the even path, the sure ground, the safety waiting there.

How can you be sure the rope will hold, the footsteps will lead to safety, the heart will not fail? Courage is required, and trust in the carver of each foothold and in the sturdiness of the rope. Faith that what lies above is worth the climb.

For some, courage comes easily. Others find it easier with the companionship of one who will ensure that their feet will not slip. For some the pathway is too daunting, but no less faith is required, no less courage, no less trust, for those who are carried.

The most daunting moments require the greatest courage—the kind of courage that helps you to allow the Deliverer to lift you off your feet and carry you over the place you cannot go. To trust in the strength of the One who lifts. To have faith that He will not fail you. —EBF

Reflect and Respond

How has He carried you over the places you cannot go?

Your favorite scripture in Psalm 17

PSALM 23:1

**The Lord is my shepherd;
I shall not want.**

The Lord refers to His people as sheep more than one hundred times in scripture, and that is not necessarily a compliment. Sheep are pretty helpless without a shepherd to watch over them. They are not the smartest of creatures and need someone to guide them to where they can find food and drink—otherwise they would likely starve. They are also fairly defenseless, an easy target for most predators. Sheep are naturally prone to wander. They will follow other sheep into darkness or danger and are very absentminded about where they are going and how to return back. When they are out and about, they can also become "cast." When a sheep is cast, it means it has flipped over on its back and is usually not able to flip itself right side up without some assistance.

Yes, sheep are very needy animals. Much like us, I suppose. Most of us easily wander or get ourselves into trouble we cannot get out of. We are helpless and hopeless without a shepherd.

Before David was king, he spent his days as a shepherd. He knew all too well the constant care and concern it takes to watch over a flock. When writing this psalm of praise about the Lord, he decided to call Him his shepherd. He knew Him as One who leads, restores, protects, and comforts. One who prepares the greatest for him and pours out all His love constantly. As His humble little sheep, David was quick to say, "Surely goodness and mercy shall follow me all the days of my life" (Psalm 23:6), especially with God leading him along. —DB

Reflect and Respond

How has the Lord been a shepherd for you?

Your favorite
scripture in
Psalm 23

PSALM 27:1

The Lord is my light and my salvation; . . . the Lord is the strength of my life; of whom shall I be afraid?

Many years ago, a group of my friends found themselves lost and stranded up in the mountain forests after a long day of snowmobiling. With all of the snow and trees looking so similar, they got turned around in the back country and were not sure how to find the path back home. They kept blazing new trails and trying to find their way, but once the sun started to set, they knew they couldn't go any farther. They sent a distress call on their satellite phone and tried to find the best place to wait out the night. Luckily, they found shelter under some trees and immediately began cutting up any branches they could find to make a fire. As the cold night settled in, they gathered around the fire for warmth, safety, and comfort. One of the friends told me afterwards that as they sat around the blazing flames, their spirits were high, and they were joking and laughing. As the fire would go down, they would get more quiet, and their spirits would start to deflate. It was as if their hope would rise and fall with the strength of the flames. They felt safe and protected in the light.

It is little wonder that David would call the Lord both his light and his salvation. He lived during some troubling days and times in his kingdom. There were moments of darkness, fear, and cold. But he knew where to turn for light, courage, and warmth.

There is a lot of cold, dark, and worry in this unpredictable world for all of us. But that same light of the Lord can burn brightly for us as it did for David. In the blaze of His presence, strength, and glory, what is there to fear? —DB

Reflect and Respond

In what ways has the Lord lit up the darkness for you?

Your favorite scripture in Psalm 27

PSALM 34:3

**O magnify the Lord with me,
and let us exalt his name together.**

King David was a gatherer of people. He gathered them to worship, to celebrate, to build, and to fight in the name of the Lord. He didn't just magnify the Lord, he brought others also to magnify and exalt His name together.

During the stormy season several years ago, a large hurricane rested over the city of Houston and poured out relentless amounts of rain for days and days on end. My parents, whose home is in Houston, were given a thirty-minute warning to grab whatever they could and get out of the city as quickly as possible. They escaped their neighborhood just as the floodwaters came rushing in. Once the storm dissipated, they returned to their home to find it completely destroyed. All of their possessions were floating in four feet of water. Their spirits were crushed. As they looked up and down the streets, every home was in the same condition.

Soon, they were overwhelmed in a new kind of way. The next day, car after car full of friends and family members and strangers showed up with shovels, power tools, and willing hearts. They stayed at each home until the work was done and then moved on to the next house. That group of people gave not only hope but a reassurance about the goodness and love of God.

I can almost hear the relief workers saying to each other as they gathered, "Come, and magnify the Lord with me, and let us exalt his name together." —DB

Reflect and Respond

When has the goodness of others helped to magnify the goodness of God to you?

Your favorite scripture in Psalm 34

PSALM 40:5

Many, O Lord my God, are thy wonderful works which thou hast done . . . more than can be numbered.

It is hard to know at what point in David's life he wrote this particular psalm, but by the time he wrote it, he had enough years under his belt to talk about some of the experiences he had been through. He wrote of days when he had needed to wait patiently on the Lord. I wonder when I read that line what he was waiting and hoping for. There seemed to be other days when he cried out to Him in trouble or sadness. For a man of war dealing with the troubles of running a kingdom, the betrayal of people closest to him, and his own temptations, I can only imagine how many nights he spent crying out.

Somewhere along the way, he found himself in a "horrible pit" of muddy clay that God had lifted him out of onto solid footing. There were days when he was lost, and the Lord "established [his] goings" and set him on his path again (Psalm 40:2). As he looked back over all his days, I imagine he could have counted everything that went wrong or bad. Seems like it was a list that would add up quickly. Instead, David looked back through all of his trouble and decided to count the goodness of God instead. As much hard as there was, the wonderful works of God were what he saw as he remembered his life. There were so many, David didn't think he would ever be able to number them. In all of his heartache, pain, and moments of loss, he saw God. In all of the good, beautiful, and hopeful days, he saw Him there, too.

There is something healing and sweet about looking for the marvelous works of God in our lives. There is also something overwhelming about it—for when we start to count it up, we lose track, and we find ourselves amazed at how good He actually is. —DB

Reflect and Respond

What are just a few of the marvelous works of God you have seen recently?

Your favorite scripture in Psalm 40

PSALM 46:1

**God is our refuge and strength,
a very present help in trouble.**

I look forward to the Second Coming of Jesus like I look forward to Christmas Day. I cannot wait for Him to come to this world again and rule as King of kings and Lord of lords. I look forward to living and working in a place where the devil does not have any influence. My heart anticipates this day more and more. I also look forward to all of His promised blessings being fulfilled. There are many things that we all might be looking forward to: not just our problems being solved and our happiness restored, but also His very presence. Often, when we talk about living the gospel of Jesus Christ, we talk about these coming blessings. We refer to His gifts in a future tense. "Someday . . ." we say.

I most certainly believe in a time to come that will be rich and overflowing with blessings that we do not currently enjoy. There are, indeed, promises that will not be fulfilled until heaven, so I will continue to hope and look forward to them with vigor and fervor. But I also hope that while we are looking to a future Jesus, we are also noticing One who is present. "A very present help in trouble" (Psalm 46:1). Life on earth can feel like a battle zone. President Boyd K. Packer once said that we are "growing up in enemy territory."[20] The blessings of the Lord are not only available in the future but can be claimed right now. He is a refuge and a strength for these current times. A refuge is a place you run to for safety *during* a time of conflict—not *after* it. He is not just the light at the end of the tunnel, He is also the light and the strength that we can enjoy and call upon as we walk through the tunnel. —DB

Reflect and Respond

When has God been a refuge and a strength for you in your ongoing battles?

Your favorite scripture in Psalm 46

PSALM 65:10

Thou makest it soft with showers:
thou blessest the springing thereof.

It has rained. For two days I have watched the gray clouds gather, felt the north wind blow, and smelled the spring cleaning that is taking place outside my windows. But more important, I have been keeping a careful eye on the raspberries my daughters and I transplanted just before the rain began. This weather has been just exactly right for raspberry transplants. The heaven-sent watering settled the furrows, made soft the soil, allowed for growth.

My constant prayer over those raspberry shoots since the afternoon my daughters and I transplanted them has been that the conditions would be exactly what they needed to take root. To grow. To thrive. "Thou visitest the earth, and waterest it. . . . Thou waterest the ridges thereof abundantly: thou settlest the furrows thereof: thou makest it soft with showers: thou blessest the springing thereof" (Psalm 65:9–10).

As I read that verse, my prayer changes from raspberries to daughters. From bare roots to gospel roots. I look to the heavens. Might He send rain in the form of inspiration, to water my daughters' souls abundantly, to settle the furrows, to make their hearts soft?

Because I see the young and tender roots there.

Tonight, this is the prayer of a mother's heart: may the Lord bless the springing thereof. —EBF

Reflect and Respond
Where has He settled the furrows and blessed the springing up in your life?

Your favorite scripture in
Psalm 65

PSALM 66:20

**Blessed be God, which hath not turned away
my prayer, nor his mercy from me.**

"For thou, O God, hast proved us: thou hast tried us, as silver is tried. . . . We went through fire and through water: but thou broughtest us out into a wealthy place. . . . Come and hear, all ye that fear God, and I will declare what he hath done for my soul. . . . Blessed be God, which hath not turned away my prayer, nor his mercy from me" (Psalm 66:10–20).

Sometimes when I read the book of Psalms, something tugs on my heartstrings. Memories mostly, of times of trial, days when I was pushed to my limit, almost to giving up. We all have "no, never" moments when we face what seems to be the worst thing. A good friend once taught me that what might seem at first to be the worst thing sometimes turns out in the end to be the best thing. It all depends on what you're looking for. Because isn't the best thing whatever leads us to know the Lord? To lean on Him? To cry unto Him? If we look carefully, we will recognize that the Lord has been with us through it all. Is that what helps turn the "no, never" moments into "I would never choose to give this up" moments?

I have a good friend whose kindergarten son slipped on the ice at recess and broke the bone next to his shoulder. What started as a trip to the emergency room for a broken bone turned into a year of visits to the oncology department at Primary Children's Hospital. I watched my friend carefully as she faced this "no, never" moment head-on. I have seen what the refiner's fire has done to her faith, her hope, her charity. She is strong enough to walk through fire and through water, through whatever is necessary to help her child. She knows and trusts the Refiner. This "no, never" place has made her wealthy in Him. —EBF

Reflect and Respond

How have you found strength through the Lord's mercy?

Your favorite scripture in **Psalm 66**

PSALM 73:23

Nevertheless I am continually with thee: thou has holden me by my right hand.

On Friday morning at 5:00 I left my home for the Salt Lake City airport. I was supposed to be traveling to Harrisburg, Pennsylvania, with seven other women. At 6:40 a.m. we boarded the plane. At 7:00 a.m. it taxied away from the terminal. At 7:15 a.m. it taxied back. Mechanical problems. We were asked to leave the plane. We couldn't help but panic. Eight of us stood in a circle, wondering what we should do now. In less than ten hours, 1200 women would gather in Harrisburg to hear us speak. But how would we get across the country in less than ten hours?

From our circle we watched the huge crowd of passengers line up at the ticket counter. Somehow we knew neither the agents there nor the customer service reps on the phone would be a resource for us. We needed heaven's help. So we turned to the Lord in prayer.

Within minutes we learned of a flight going to the East Coast, currently boarding passengers, on the other side of the airport. We started to run. We were guaranteed two seats on the plane, but we needed six more. Again, we turned to the Lord. Somehow, within minutes, all eight of us stood in line. Eight women with eight tickets for a flight to the East Coast.

Somehow. What started out as a flight to Harrisburg, Pennsylvania, turned into a flight to Washington, DC, and still our hearts were focused on the goal—Pennsylvania.

After a four-hour plane ride and a three-and-a-half-hour car ride, we made it. We were directed each step of the way, with strangers somehow placed in our path to assist us, through heaven's help. *Somehow.* I know how it happened: We were held by the right hand, guided from heaven, because we put our trust in the Lord. —EBF

Reflect and Respond

When have you experienced a miracle after putting your trust in the Lord?

Your favorite scripture in Psalm 73

PSALM 77:12-13

I will meditate also of all thy work, and talk of thy doings. Thy way, O God, is in the sanctuary.

We live in a very noisy and quick-moving world. It seems like our lives get busier and busier with each passing year. People of the past seemed to have the luxury of moments of solitude more abundantly than we do today. There used to be this thing called spare time.

Today, we don't seem to have any time to ourselves or our thoughts. Instead of escaping the world, we usually take it with us on a phone or other device in our pockets or purses. And whenever and wherever there is a dull moment, we pull that device out and get distracted: at a stoplight, or sitting in the doctor's office, or waiting in line at the grocery store. All of this leads to our bodies and minds running ragged and makes it almost impossible for us to simply sit still.

I have a good friend who is an evangelical Christian who is in the middle of a very busy season of life—working, putting her husband through school, and raising two active children. Recognizing the need for a place of strength and stillness in her life, once a month, when she goes into the bigger city for things they don't have in her small town, she carves out time to visit the temple there. She doesn't have a recommend, but she asks the men in white at the front desk if she can sit in the waiting room. She takes in her Bible and spends much needed time in what she calls her "appointment with God." A time of refuge and meditation.

Perhaps in the busyness of life, we can find the time our souls need to stop, be still, think and meditate on the goodness of God, and find sanctuary in His presence. —DB

Reflect and Respond

What do you do to find stillness and sanctuary in God's presence?

Your favorite scripture in Psalm 77

PSALM 91:11-12

**For he shall give his angels charge
over thee, to . . . bear thee up.**

Have you ever had one of those moments when you are not sure if you can put one foot in front of the other? Maybe the trail has been going uphill for longer than you anticipated, or the load you carry is too heavy for one person to bear alone. Sometimes you feel it when you turn a corner only to realize the end is nowhere in sight. Your thoughts fill with doubt and discouragement. You wonder exactly why you chose this course, this journey, this destination.

"For he shall give his angels charge over thee, to keep thee in all thy ways. They shall bear thee up in their hands, lest thou dash thy foot against a stone" (Psalm 91:11–12). I believe angels are real. I know they are. Because in moments of discouragement and doubt, when I haven't the strength to put one foot in front of the other, the Lord has sent angels to bear me up.

I don't know what your circumstances are today. Perhaps you are in desperate need of heaven's help. If so, I pray the Lord will give His angels charge over thee. But even more important, I pray that He will open your eyes to recognize the angels that He sends. Angels come in different shapes and sizes, and bearing up comes in ways we might not anticipate.

But maybe your circumstances right now do not require bearing up. Perhaps, in this moment, all is well with you. If that is the case, maybe you could set aside time this week to be on the errand of angels, to share your gift.

Today might find you watching for angels, or it might find you acting as an angel. No matter what your circumstances are or where your steps may lead, may His angels keep thee. Watch over thee. Bear thee up. Today, and always. —EBF

Reflect and Respond

*What is your circumstance today? To watch for angels,
or to be an angel?*

Your favorite
scripture in
Psalm 91

PSALM 100:1

Make a joyful noise unto the Lord, all ye lands.

When I ride in my car, I turn the volume to my music up louder than most people want it to be. When we were making finishing touches to our basement, I insisted on us buying a really big subwoofer so that our chests would vibrate when we watch movies together. I adore really loud concerts. I also sing in the shower at the top of my lungs (much to the dismay of everyone else sleeping in the house at the time). And a sports arena full of fans cheering is one of my favorite settings to be in. I cannot get enough of it! Oh, and did I mention fireworks? The bigger the better! I like loud. I also value the peace and quiet, but if there is too much of it, ironically, I can't concentrate.

Most of the worship that I am involved in on a weekly, Sunday schedule is kind of quiet. I appreciate the need for this, particularly during the holy sacrament. But if I had my way, once it was over, I would be clapping in church. *Reverence* is a word that comes from *revere*. It is not a word that comes from *quiet*. Sometimes, we revere quietly, but other times, my heart yearns to "make a joyful noise unto the Lord." To sing out praises. To shout hallelujah and hosanna! I loved learning that before there were buildings available other than the temple, the Saints in the early pioneer days would dance inside the temples. Now, of course, there are times and places for quiet revering, and times and places for a joyful noise, but I believe our souls need both of them. One of my favorite quotes from Brigham Young is, "If you desire to ask God for anything, you are as well prepared to do so in the dance as in any other place, if you are Saints."[21] —DB

Reflect and Respond

What does your heart want to make a joyful noise to the Lord about?

Your favorite scripture in Psalm 100

PSALM 119:24

Thy testimonies also are my delight and my counsellors.

One of the best gifts that I have ever received is hanging, framed, in the front entry of my house. If my house were to ever burn down, I would get my wife, my kids, and that framed picture out. Everything else is replaceable. Inside the frame is a page out of a Bible. But not just any Bible—a page from a 1582 Geneva Bible. The Geneva Bible, one of the first Bibles printed in English, was instrumental in the Protestant Reformation, and it was the version of the Bible the Pilgrims brought with them to the Americas. During the time of its printing, it was illegal to have a copy of the Bible in English, so it was printed in Switzerland and then often smuggled across the borders. Many people were willing, and many people did die trying to get the words of the Lord from the Bible into the hands and hearts of as many people as they could.

Psalm 119 is not only the longest chapter in scripture, but it is unique because of its format. It is divided into sections that are labeled with the beginning letters of the Hebrew alphabet from first to last to suggest a completeness and fullness of thought. It is in beautiful form, but its words are the real treasure. The whole poem is a praise for and expression of gratitude to God for the words of scripture. One of my favorite lines is when the writer calls the words of scripture his or her delight and counselors. I have looked to the scriptures many times for advice and counsel. They have also cheered up my heart and brought great delight to me. I will forever be thankful to a long line of people who sacrificed greatly so those words could be so available to me today. —DB

Reflect and Respond
What do you find most valuable about scripture in your life?

Your favorite scripture in **Psalm 119**

PSALM 126:5

They that sow in tears shall reap in joy.

I learned a powerful lesson one summer from my friend Mary Ellen Edmunds that left an image in my heart that I won't ever forget. Many years ago, just after the fall of 2004, an amazing phenomenon happened in Death Valley, a parched desert country just outside of Baker, California. The mountains that surround this desert country are formed in such a way that the hot air recirculates throughout the valley, making this area one of the hottest places on earth. On some summer afternoons the ground-level temperatures can reach up to 200 degrees.

The flowers in this desert country are unique in the fact that the seeds they produce have an extra thick, waxy coating that allows them to hibernate on the desert floor for decades. The particular seeds that covered the ground in the fall of 2004 had weathered years of severe extremes as they waited, dormant, on the desert floor.

And then, an early winter rainstorm came late in the fall. The rainstorms continued at regular intervals throughout the winter and into spring. This deep-soaking, gentle rain was essential. It began to wash away the protective covering that surrounded the seeds, and with time, they began to sprout.

In the spring of 2005, six inches of rain fell on the thirsty desert floor—three times the usual amount for this hot country. The conditions caused wildflowers that had been dormant for decades to sprout and take root across the valley floor, covering the stark white sand and black basalt mountainside with a rare burst of color that spread across Death Valley, carpeting the desert floor with vibrant pink, purple, white, and yellow wildflowers.

Experts said this kind of show is experienced just once in a lifetime. It happened because the conditions were right. Suddenly a parched desert floor was covered with petals. The rain was essential to the process, allowing what had once lain dormant to take root and sprout, until each seed eventually bloomed into a miraculous display of beauty.

Somewhere within each of us there are seeds that have been carefully placed. These seeds are waiting patiently, dormant, for their time to come. When the conditions are right, they will take root. Sometimes the perfect condition that allows for the growth of these seeds is painful. Like the rain, tears may be required. Slowly and gently, these precious tears will wash away the protective covering that surrounds the seeds, and they will begin to sprout.

There is a unique beauty found in this kind of seed, for it blooms into a rare and precious blossom—one that you will treasure and protect, one that you will share with others when the conditions are right, one that would have lain dormant for your entire lifetime without this particular moment to allow for its growth.

The Lord knew about these kinds of seeds. He spoke of those who would tend carefully to their growth. "They that sow in tears shall reap in joy. He that goeth forth and weepeth, bearing precious seed, shall doubtless come again with rejoicing, bringing his sheaves with him" (Psalm 126:5–6). The Lord will attend us through this sowing process, and often after the tears are dried we will discover that the precious seed we bore has blossomed into something worth rejoicing over—something we might not have recognized before the tears began to fall. We must remember, "Weeping may endure for a night, but joy cometh in the morning" (Psalm 30:5). Those who sow in tears will eventually reap in joy.

That is the promise of the Lord. —EBF

Reflect and Respond

When is a time when your tears have turned to rejoicing?

Your favorite scripture in **Psalm 126**

PROVERBS 3:5

**Trust in the Lord with all thine heart; and lean
not unto thine own understanding.**

I once had a conversation with a friend about a decision I was making. From the sound of things, it appeared I was leaning heavily on my own wisdom rather than the advice and direction of the Lord. My friend asked me, "How many universes have you created?" I was taken aback. "What?" "You heard me," he said. "How many universes have you created?" My answer was obvious. "Zero." His reply: "Exactly." I am not sure how many universes God has created, but I understand what my friend was trying to say. Point made. And amen.

The book of Proverbs is known as wisdom literature. It isn't the law of the Lord that we find in the first five books, or the prophetic writings that we find in others, but rather a collection of generations of people trying to live according to God's way. The wisdom it contains is more than knowledge, but rather practical skills for living well in this world and living in awe and reverence for God. It shows a way to embrace what He knows is best. Most of the writings are attributed to King Solomon, who was given the gift of wisdom by the Lord. They cover a wide variety of topics, including work, marriage, friendships, love, generosity, anger, peace, happiness, and on and on. The proverbs are invitations to live principles, not necessarily promises. Life is tricky, complicated, and there are not many guarantees. But living according to the wisdom of God's people is most likely to lead us to peace and success.

Although there are not many guarantees in life, one thing is certain—God's heart. It is good. And we can trust in it with all of ours. We can safely lean into His understanding and wisdom instead of our own. It is sturdy and sure. —DB

Reflect and Respond

When do you find it difficult to trust in the Lord and lean into His understanding?

Your favorite scripture in
Proverbs 3

PROVERBS 6:16

**These six things doth the Lord hate: yea, seven
are an abomination unto him . . .**

Chapter 6 of Proverbs lists a number of things the Lord hates:

1. A proud look
2. A lying tongue
3. Hands that shed innocent blood
4. A heart that deviseth wicked imaginations
5. Feet that be swift in running to mischief
6. A false witness that speaketh lies (that is, slander or gossip)
7. He that soweth discord among brethren

On that list of things the Lord hates, the last two stand out to me. Their lessons have caused me to ponder. It has never occurred to me that one can be called a false witness for spreading gossip, rumors, or slander—but it is such a good description. My mind has also been caught up on what it means to sow discord. When we were little, my dad would always counsel us not to "stir the pot." That was the first phrase that came to mind when I read the words "soweth discord."

A good definition for *discord* is "lack of harmony." I play the piano, and I love learning songs that stretch my ability. But sometimes the level of difficulty within a song will lead to my fingers landing on the wrong notes within a chord. Just that one wrong chord can ruin the entire piece. That is how powerful discord is.

I've also been considering how looking to the opposite of something the Lord hates could lead to a quality the Lord would love. What if we took the seven things the Lord hates and learned to live the exact opposite of those qualities instead?

1. A humble view
2. A truthful speech
3. Hands that protect and nurture
4. A heart that deviseth wise thoughts

5. Feet that be swift in running to good
6. A true witness that speaks compliments
7. He that spreads harmony among brethren

Seven areas I need to work on. Seven things I could be better at. Starting now. —EBF

Reflect and Respond
Which of the things the Lord hates would you like to try living the opposite of?

Your favorite scripture in
Proverbs 6

PROVERBS 17:17

**A friend loveth at all times,
and a brother is born for adversity.**

Josh was in fourth grade and Caleb was in sixth. They were getting ready upstairs when the banging began, and the yelling. *What could they be arguing about at this time of day?* I wondered. But as I arrived at the bottom of the stairs, I realized it wasn't an argument but an emergency—the one we had planned for but prayed would never happen. Josh, in a diabetic hypoglycemic state of unawareness, had climbed into the bathtub where Caleb was bathing, slipped under the water, and started having a seizure. Caleb, the older brother caught unaware, had reached his arms under Josh and lifted his head and shoulders out of the water. Then he began calling my name. I will never forget his tiny frame being knocked violently against the waterspout as he held Josh above the water with all his might until I came running frantically up the stairs and pulled Josh out of the water onto the bathroom floor. I won't forget the red marks already bruising along Caleb's spine. I won't forget listening to my twelve-year-old on the phone trying to direct the ambulance to our home while I gave Josh a shot filled with sugar, made sure he continued to breathe, held him so he wouldn't hurt himself. I won't forget Caleb standing over his brother as the paramedics came. Silent. Watching. He wouldn't leave for school until he knew his brother was safe. That was the memory that filled my mind when I read this verse, "A friend loveth at all times, and a brother is born for adversity" (Proverbs 17:17).

Wouldn't it be a blessing if we could all learn to be that kind of friend? The kind who lifts another who is drowning, who seeks the help that will bring healing, who provides watch care, and companionship, and loyalty. A friend who loveth at all times. —EBF

Reflect and Respond

How could you help bear up someone through their adversity?

Your favorite
scripture in
Proverbs 17

PROVERBS 22:1

A good name is rather to be chosen than great riches.

Each of my children was named after someone they can look up to. My husband, Greg, and I felt just as Helaman did when he explained to his sons Lehi and Nephi, "Behold, I have given unto you the names of our first parents who came out of the land of Jerusalem; and this I have done that when you remember your names ye may remember them; . . . and when ye remember their works ye may know how that it is said, and also written, that they were good. Therefore, my sons, I would that ye should do that which is good, that it may be said of you, and also written, even as it has been said and written of them" (Helaman 5:6–7). Our children enjoy hearing the stories behind why we chose each of their names.

In our home we have a framed statement that reads, "Be true to who you are, and the family name you bear." Shortly after we hung the quote, we talked about what it meant to be true to a name. We wanted our kids to remember that everything they do, both inside and outside of our home, represents the entire family. Their choices determine whether or not they bring honor to our family, and also to the person they were named after.

Then we talked about another important name each of us has been given: the name of Jesus Christ. King Benjamin said, "Therefore, I would that ye should take upon you the name of Christ . . . and it shall come to pass that whosoever doeth this shall be found at the right hand of God, for he shall know the name by which he is called; for he shall be called by the name of Christ" (Mosiah 5:8–9). Every week, as we partake of the sacrament, we covenant to take His name. If a good name is rather to be chosen than riches, then His is the best name of all. —EBF

Reflect and Respond
What does taking His name mean to you?

Your favorite scripture in Proverbs 22

PROVERBS 31:10

Who can find a virtuous woman?

Often when we read Proverbs 31, we begin at verse 10, "Who can find a virtuous woman?" However, the proverb becomes even more meaningful if we begin with verse one. This chapter begins with a mother seeking to counsel her son who will one day be king. The bulk of her counsel becomes a description of a woman with strong character, wisdom, skills, and compassion. Perhaps this mother wanted her son to find a woman who would enable him to reach his highest potential as she sought to discover her own.

I just can't help but ponder the power of qualities like these:

- her price is far above rubies
- she considereth a field . . . and planteth a vineyard
- her candle goeth not out by night
- strength and honour are her clothing
- she openeth her mouth with wisdom
- she shall rejoice in a time to come

When I read words such as *trust, worketh, riseth, considereth, strengtheneth, perceiveth, stretcheth, reacheth, maketh, openeth,* and *looketh*, I can't help but look back and remember the women who have been influential in my life—my mother, aunts, grandmothers, sisters, friends, and ministers. Women who have enabled me to recognize my great potential because they have embraced theirs. Who can find a virtuous woman? Hopefully each of our lives has been filled to overflowing with them, and one day I hope to be considered as one. —EBF

Reflect and Respond

What is your favorite description from Proverbs 31?

Your favorite scripture in **Proverbs 31**

ECCLESIASTES 7:8

Better is the end of a thing than the beginning thereof...

Have you ever found the end of a thing to be the best part? The end of a really good book, the last bite of a Snickers candy bar, the final score of a game your team just won. Those are the kind of endings I am talking about. As I was thinking about good endings, I realized we are almost at the end of the Old Testament, which is a remarkable thought.

It's been a good year. We have come to admire scripture heroes we have heard of but never really studied before—Abraham, Moses, Joshua, Deborah, Gideon, Hannah, the Great Woman, Leah, Jehoshaphat, Micaiah, David, and Mephibosheth, to name a few. Along the way we have discovered lessons we hadn't learned before, gathered the promises to covenant Israel, and come to better understand the role of Jehovah, the Deliverer.

Perhaps the Old Testament has not been quite as intimidating as you had imagined it would be. Maybe you have fallen in love with this book of scripture that may have felt daunting at first. I think you will find that the ending will be better than the beginning.

I just can't stop thinking of how we have been so richly blessed already.

And yet, there is more. —EBF

Reflect and Respond

What has been your favorite part of the Old Testament so far?

Your favorite scripture in **Ecclesiastes 7**

ISAIAH 1:1

The vision of Isaiah the son of Amoz...

Perhaps you grew up in the same generation that I did. It's the one in which every-one told you to skip the Isaiah chapters when you read the Book of Mormon. When you wondered why, those same people told you that you wouldn't be able to understand them. Perhaps you believed them. If that has been your experience, then I am going to ask you to set that all aside.

Lots of times people think they don't like peas, or avocados, or crème brûlée. And then they try the thing they thought they hated—*really try it*—and find out after all this time that they actually like those things a lot. There is thanksgiving that comes in those moments, gratitude for the simple fact that you won't go through the rest of your life missing out on something you didn't know you were going to love so much.

So, in preparation for the beginning of Isaiah, let me share with you five reasons why I love Isaiah.

1. "... that I might more fully persuade them to believe in the Lord their Redeemer I did read unto them that which was written by the prophet Isaiah" (1 Nephi 19:23). One of the things I love most about Isaiah is his testimony of the Lord. He has a beautiful way of expressing his belief in the Savior. It is poetic, and visual, and he teaches us character-istics of the Lord in a way that is different from any other book of scripture. **As you read Isaiah this time, watch for verses that testify of Christ. Mark them. Learn from them.**

2. "Surely he spake as touching all things. . . . All things that he spake have been and shall be, even according to the words which he spake" (3 Nephi 23:1–3). I love that Isaiah "spake as touching all things" . . . and it is true. Within these pages you will find his testimony of many gospel principles, including tithing, fast offerings, the Atonement of Jesus Christ, the Church in the latter days, the stakes of Zion, and the temple, among others. **This time when you read Isaiah, watch for verses that speak counsel, and also verses that speak warning. What can you learn from them?**

3. "In the days that the prophecies of Isaiah shall be fulfilled men shall know of a

surety, at the times when they shall come to pass" (2 Nephi 25:7). The book of Isaiah contains many prophecies, some of which have already come to pass, and others which are still before us. **As you read Isaiah, watch for prophecies—both those that have been fulfilled and those that will be.**

4. "They shall be of great worth unto them in the last days; for in that day shall they understand them; wherefore, for their good have I written them" (2 Nephi 25:8). Nephi has given us a great promise: we live in the last days, which means we are the people who will understand the words of Isaiah. What an incredible gift—to be able to understand. **This time as you read the words of Isaiah, pray for the Spirit to be with you, then have faith in the promise given by Nephi: you *will* understand them.**

5. "Search these things diligently; for great are the words of Isaiah" (3 Nephi 23:1). The words of Isaiah are great. This is something I believe with all my heart. Take your time. Read slowly. Soak it in. Watch for the imagery. Get caught up in the poetry. **As you turn each page of this sacred text, remind yourself of that truth: *great* are the words of Isaiah. Believe it, and it will be so.** —EBF

Reflect and Respond

What are you looking forward to most about Isaiah?

Your favorite scripture in
Isaiah 1

ISAIAH 4:5-6

**...for upon all the glory shall be a defence
...and for a place of refuge...**

As you read Isaiah, it helps to create images in your mind of what the verses are describing. As each image is visualized, the message from Isaiah becomes more clear. Consider Isaiah 4:5–6. Maybe you could read it like this:

And the Lord will create upon every *home*
and upon every *congregation*
divine protection by day,
and *the presence of God* by night: for defense.
And there shall be a *temple*
for a place of refuge, for *relief,* for *shelter,*
from the *storms of life,* from the *intensity,* from the *constant battle.*

What do you see? What do you learn?

My *testimony* of the Lord is strengthened as I trust His promise to create protection, defense, and refuge. I recognize the *counsel* within those verses, and I am reminded of the importance of preparing myself to be always worthy to visit the temple—for it is there that I will find the refuge, the relief, and the shelter He has promised. I see the *prophecy* of the promise of the Lord to offer divine protection in the last days, and I am grateful to live in the time that Isaiah is speaking of. I *feel the Spirit helping me to understand* the truthfulness of Isaiah's words through the imagery, through the beauty of the language, and through the footnotes at the bottom of the page. Within those two verses I experience the *greatness* of the words of Isaiah. —EBF

Reflect and Respond

Why do you think visualizing Isaiah's words would help you to understand them better?

Your favorite scripture in Isaiah 4

ISAIAH 14:3

Rest . . . from the hard bondage
wherein thou wast made to serve.

When you think of the word *yoke*, you probably think of the wooden yoke with two sides, used by a pair of oxen. But have you ever seen a single yoke? This type of yoke is made of leather and used by a horse required to pull an oppressive or burdensome load.

It is the thickness that strikes me first. The yoke has been crafted to withstand intense pressure, maximum loads, exhaustive work. *I do not ever want to be yoked to something that is oppressive or burdensome.* I focus on the details, the imagery, and I think of my life.

Perhaps you and I are not yoked to heavy equipment meant to be dragged through fields or furrows. But do we know the oppression of being yoked in our world today? I think of those who are burdened by debt, by addiction, by sorrow, by health conditions, or by fear. Sometimes life requires us to shoulder a heavy load—one we might not have chosen but from which we cannot get free. If we are yoked to this type of burden, or if someone who is dear to us shoulders this kind of load, we must remember that all is not lost. "And it shall come to pass in that day, that *his* burden shall be taken away from off thy shoulder, and *his* yoke from off thy neck, and the yoke shall be destroyed *because of the anointing*" (Isaiah 10:27; emphasis added).

Because of the anointing.

The Bible Dictionary explains that "the English word *Christ* is from a Greek word meaning 'anointed' and is the equivalent of *Messiah*, which is from a Hebrew and Aramaic term meaning 'anointed'" (Bible Dictionary, "Anointed One"). There *is* One who can give us rest from bondage, One who can remove the yoke. The Anointed One.

"The Spirit of the Lord God is upon me; because the Lord hath anointed me to preach good tidings unto the meek; he hath sent me to bind up the brokenhearted, to proclaim liberty to the captives, and the opening of the prison to them that are bound; . . . to comfort all that mourn; . . . to give unto them beauty for ashes, the oil of joy for mourning, the garment of praise for the spirit of heaviness" (Isaiah 61:1–3).

He is Jesus Christ, the Holy One of Israel, the Anointed One. He offers rest. Relief from oppression. He will make our burdens light (see Matthew 11:30).

"And it shall come to pass . . . that the Lord shall give thee rest from thy sorrow, and from thy fear, and from the hard bondage wherein thou wast made to serve" (Isaiah 14:3).

Are you in bondage? Do you know someone who is yoked to something oppressive or burdensome? Turn to the Lord. The Anointed One. Jesus Christ. The Messiah. The yoke will be destroyed *because* of the anointing.

Because of Him.

Through Him. —EBF

Reflect and Respond

How have you found rest from the Lord in moments of great bondage?

Your favorite scripture in
Isaiah 14

ISAIAH 22:11

Ye have not looked unto the maker thereof...

Michelangelo's *Pietà* is a statue of Mary, the mother of Jesus, holding her son after the Crucifixion. Something unique about this sculpture is that it is the only work Michelangelo ever signed. There is a story that surrounds the signing of Michelangelo's name told by his good friend Giorgio Vasari. Shortly after the sculpture went on display, it is said that Michelangelo overheard someone remark that Michelangelo could not have sculpted it—he was too young. People said it was the work of another sculptor, Cristoforo Solari. After hearing this remark, in the late hours of the night, Michelangelo chiseled one sentence onto Mary's sash: *Michaelangelus Bonarotus Florentinus Facibat* ("Michelangelo Buonarroti, Florentine, made this"). It is said that Michelangelo later regretted his pride in that moment and vowed never to sign another work.

There is much I love about this story. I am impressed that Michelangelo was able to convey so much emotion about the sacrifice of Christ in a piece of art at such a young age. Surely his testimony is captured within the beauty of the work. I love that, should there be any doubt as to the validity of the testimony sculpted by his hands, he signed his name. *Michelangelo made this.* I find it remarkable that the only work Michelangelo ever signed was his testimony of the Atonement of Christ. This story reminds me that I want to be willing to sign my name to what I know to be true even when people don't believe my testimony. *Emily Freeman believes this.* I want my life to reflect my belief.

But there is a deeper lesson we learn; it is taught in the words of Isaiah. "Surely your turning of things upside down shall be esteemed as the potter's clay: for shall the work say of him that made it, He made me not?" (Isaiah 29:16). I can't help but remember those who questioned the skill of the maker who created the *Pietà,* of Michelangelo, of his ability. Now my thoughts turn higher. I think of the Master, the Creator, the Maker, and wonder how many of us question our own worth in the hands of the Potter. Isaiah gives us a profound reminder: "Ye have not looked unto the maker thereof, neither had respect unto him that fashioned it long ago" (Isaiah 22:11). The footnote next to the word *maker* explains, "you have not turned to the Lord."

I am reminded of the days when I question my worth, my abilities, my importance. What does the Maker think to Himself on those days? Does He wish He could reach down with His fingertip and somehow remind me, "Jesus Christ made this"? Oh, if we could only see our worth in His eyes! If only we could understand the potential He has in mind for us. If only we could visualize the beauty of His work in each one of us, individually. If only we would allow Him to shape us and mold us into who He knows we can be.

What if, on our darkest days, we remembered to look unto the Maker? How different would our perspective be?

"At that day shall a man look to his Maker, and his eyes shall have respect to the Holy One of Israel" (Isaiah 17:7). —EBF

Reflect and Respond

What would you see if you viewed your potential from His eyes today?

Your favorite scripture in Isaiah 22

ISAIAH 35:8

And it shall be called The way of holiness . . .

One weekend I accepted an invitation to walk the twenty-four miles from the Draper Utah Temple to the Salt Lake Temple. We left the Draper Temple at 7:00 a.m. Our walk began with a quote from J. Golden Kimball: "When I think about [the temple], every stone in it is a sermon to me. It tells of suffering, it tells of sacrifice, it preaches—every rock in it, preaches a discourse. . . . Every window, every steeple, everything about the Temple speaks of the things of God, and gives evidence of the faith of the people who built it."[22] We were reminded about the stone on the Salt Lake Temple that John Moyle carved after walking to the temple on an artificial leg. *Holiness to the Lord.* That stone became the evidence of his faith. *Holiness to the Lord* became his sermon.

As we walked, we each asked ourselves, "What is *my* sermon?" For the next several miles we spoke of what our individual sermons were: "Love well, serve well." "Live with no regrets." "Enjoy every moment." "Talk of Christ." "Stand as a witness." "Kindness matters."

In the afternoon, as we neared the end, we became footsore and weary. We looked to each other for strength. The conversation turned deeper; we spoke of what it meant to be holy. From the Bible Dictionary we learned that things that were considered holy were set apart for a sacred purpose. We began to realize that if we want our life to be holy, then it must be set apart, consecrated, for a sacred purpose. We considered what that holy purpose might be. Brigham Young counseled, "Every moment of my life must be holiness to the Lord."[23]

Every moment of my life must be *set apart* to the Lord. *Consecrated* to the Lord.

Now, as we walked, we spoke of holiness. I looked around the group of people we were walking with. Everyone in the group had shown up that morning in exercise clothing: running shoes, sweatshirts. Every person except one. This boy unexpectedly showed up in a kilt. It was in the last few miles that I heard his story. He made that kilt all by himself—ordered the fabric straight from Scotland. He had decided the kilt would be worn only on special occasions, and when he woke up that morning, he knew the day was going to be special. It would be a day he wanted to always remember. It qualified for wearing the kilt. A day set apart, consecrated, holy.

"And an highway shall be there, and a way, and it shall be called The way of holiness; . . . but it shall be for those: the wayfaring men . . . the redeemed shall walk there . . . and come to Zion with songs and everlasting joy upon their heads: they shall obtain joy and gladness, and sorrow and sighing shall flee away" (Isaiah 35:8–10).

Next, I spoke with a girl who moved to Utah from Peru one week before the walk. She heard about the walk on her first Sunday here, and she wanted to come. She explained that this would be her very first time to see the Salt Lake Temple. She knew she would never forget it.

On mile twenty-two, I walked behind two brothers. One brother could barely lift his foot to take another step, it was so blistered. But giving up was not an option. The other brother matched his stride step for step, speaking softly words of confidence, hand on back to steady, to offer strength, ensuring he would reach the end. "Strengthen ye the weak hands, and confirm the feeble knees. Say to them that are of a fearful heart, Be strong, fear not" (Isaiah 35:3–4).

There is something remarkable that happens when you walk the way of holiness. You learn things about people you never knew before. You learn things about yourself you never knew before. This way of holiness is not meant for everyone. It tells of suffering and sacrifice. Every step gives evidence of the faith of the person who walks it. —EBF

Reflect and Respond
What does it look like to walk in holiness?

Your favorite scripture in Isaiah 35

ISAIAH 43:4-5

Since thou wast precious in my sight . . . I have loved thee. . . . Fear not: for I am with thee.

Sometimes you just need to know the Lord is near because the journey seems long. Although the scenery is breathtaking and the companions pleasant, there are moments when you might wonder if you can take another step. It could be that you're not quite ready for the detour, or the change of course, or the incline that lies ahead. In those moments, I find myself reaching out for the One whose companionship becomes a lifeline. My favorite scripture passage is a reminder of the truth that He is with us through every wilderness place. It is a scripture I have carried in my heart through the worst days. It has gotten me through the longest nights. It has brought peace through the times of heartache. —EBF

But now thus saith the Lord that created thee . . .
fear not: for I have redeemed thee,
I have called thee by thy name;
thou art mine.
When thou passest through the waters, I will be with thee;
and through the rivers, they shall not overflow thee:
when thou walkest through the fire, thou shalt not be burned;
neither shall the flame kindle upon thee.
For I am the Lord thy God, the Holy One of Israel, thy Saviour. . . .
Since thou wast precious in my sight . . . I have loved thee. . . .
Fear not: for I am with thee. (Isaiah 43:1–5)

Reflect and Respond

What is it about that scripture that brings comfort to you?

Your favorite scripture in Isaiah 43

ISAIAH 49:5

My God shall be my strength.

When our son Caleb was serving his mission in Croatia, a General Authority came and spoke at a mission conference. He explained that the scriptures are a book of evidences—a record kept by the children of the Lord of the moments when they witnessed His hand in their lives. He invited the missionaries to purchase a notebook and start keeping their own Book of Evidences. That Christmas, I bought each of my kids an inexpensive leather journal with "Book of Evidences" imprinted on the cover. I challenged my family to start keeping a record of our dealings with the Lord: prayers answered, moments when the Spirit was felt, experiences when they knew the Lord was aware of their story.

Isaiah is one of the prophets who kept a book of evidences. His witnesses are powerful: "I will pour water upon him that is thirsty, and floods upon the dry ground: I will pour my spirit upon thy seed" (Isaiah 44:3). "Remember . . . I have formed thee; . . . thou shalt not be forgotten of me" (Isaiah 44:21). "I will go before thee, and make the crooked places straight" (Isaiah 45:2). "I have raised him up in righteousness, and I will direct all his ways" (Isaiah 45:13). "I have spoken it, I will also bring it to pass; I have purposed it, I will also do it" (Isaiah 46:11). "Behold, I have refined thee, but not with silver; I have chosen thee in the furnace of affliction" (Isaiah 48:10). "My God shall be my strength" (Isaiah 49:5).

As we write down these moments, these experiences, these memories, our faith in the Lord will be strengthened. Perhaps page after page will become filled with our testimony, just as the pages of Isaiah are filled with his. —EBF

Reflect and Respond

What is one experience you would record in your own Book of Evidences?

Your favorite scripture in
Isaiah 49

ISAIAH 58:11

A spring of water, whose waters fail not.

When I was young, my family would visit Cascade Springs at the top of American Fork Canyon. We walked along small rivers and past waterfalls until we reached the higher ground where we found the wellspring—a place where the water flowed out of seemingly impermeable rock before it began cascading down the mountain. The water never stopped; there was an overflowing fullness.

Every time I read chapter 58 of Isaiah, I think about Cascade Springs. I love the four reasons for fasting defined here: to loose the bands of wickedness, to undo the heavy burdens, to let the oppressed go free, and to break every yoke. We are also reminded of the importance of fast offerings in relation to the law of the fast: to deal thy bread to the hungry, to remember the poor, and the naked, and those within our circle of influence who are struggling (Isaiah 58:6–7). Then we read about the blessings: light, health, righteousness, the Lord as our rearward. "Then shalt thou call, and the Lord shall answer; thou shalt cry, and he shall say, Here I am" (Isaiah 58:8–9).

Next comes the verse that reminds me so much of Cascade Springs: "And the Lord shall guide thee continually, and satisfy thy soul in drought, and make fat thy bones: *and thou shalt be like a watered garden, and like a spring of water, whose waters fail not*" (Isaiah 58:11; emphasis added). I love the thought of the Lord guiding us continually, but I especially love the image of the spring of water, whose waters fail not. An overflowing fullness. Abundance.

Every time I read this chapter, I pause for just a moment to consider the blessings of keeping the true law of the fast and the Wellspring from whence those blessings flow. —EBF

Reflect and Respond

How has the Lord been a wellspring in your life?

Your favorite scripture in
Isaiah 58

JEREMIAH 1:5

Before I formed thee in the belly I knew thee; . . .
I sanctified thee, and I ordained thee.

Jeremiah was a prophet who was called to preach in the years just before the southern kingdom was destroyed and the people were taken away as exiles into Babylon. He was one of the last prophets to warn those people about the effects of breaking their covenant relationship with God and the consequences of abandoning His protective strength. In the Book of Mormon, we learn from Lehi that the Lord sent many prophets to warn the people during this time. Although we don't know if they knew each other or not, Jeremiah and Lehi would have been contemporary prophets with each other in the city of Jerusalem (see 1 Nephi 1:4).

Sometimes I wonder what it must have felt like to be one of those prophets in a time like that. No one was listening or seemed to care, and maybe it was all in vain. Perhaps there were days when Jeremiah remembered the Lord's encouraging call to him, when He said, "Before I formed thee in the belly I knew thee; . . . I sanctified thee, and I ordained thee a prophet unto the nations" (Jeremiah 1:5). Jeremiah's call wasn't happenstance or a response from a God taken off guard. Years before Jeremiah was even born, the Lord knew what the people of Jerusalem would need. He also knew the kind of man who would be able and willing to perform the mission needed for such an awful and difficult time. Jeremiah was formed for such an occasion, sanctified and made ready, and chosen and ordained for that specific work at that specific time.

Perhaps as you consider the circumstances that you find yourself in and the mission you were called to fulfill, wondering if you match the message, you can remember a God who knew you and chose you and was making things ready even before you were born. —DB

Reflect and Respond

How does it encourage you to know you were known and sanctified before you began your work?

Your favorite scripture in Jeremiah 1

JEREMIAH 8:14

Why do we sit still?

Every time I begin reading the Book of Mormon, my imagination is stirred. I can't help but wonder about the conditions in Jerusalem during that time period. I wonder how bad the world around me would have to get before I would leave behind my home, my belongings, my neighbors, and my lifestyle to haul my children out into the wilderness and live in a tent. When I picture Lehi packing up his entire family and leaving his home and possessions, it makes me think that things in Jerusalem must have been pretty bad.

Jeremiah and Lehi would have been contemporaries. The Jerusalem Lehi left is the same Jerusalem Jeremiah is writing about in his book. As I read the words of Jeremiah, it helps me begin to understand the hardship of raising a righteous family in an increasingly wicked world. Besides the gross wickedness and sin, Jeremiah describes the Jerusalem Lehi left with words such as these: "They are not valiant for the truth . . . they know not me" (Jeremiah 9:3), "no man repented him of his wickedness" (Jeremiah 8:6), "they . . . went backward, and not forward" (Jeremiah 7:24), "this people hath . . . a rebellious heart" (Jeremiah 5:23), "families that call not on thy name" (Jeremiah 10:25), "they went after other gods to serve them" (Jeremiah 11:10).

Jeremiah describes what these other gods were like: "For one cutteth a tree out of the forest, the work of the hands of the workman, with the axe. They deck it with silver and with gold; they fasten it with nails and with hammers, *that it move not.* They are upright as the palm tree, *but speak not: . . . they cannot go.* Be not afraid of them; for they cannot do evil, neither also is it in them to do good" (Jeremiah 10:3–5; emphasis added). I find myself wondering why Israel would choose to worship a god like this—one that cannot move, speak, or go. A god that is unable to do good. Obviously, in our day we don't have a god made out of wood and decked with silver and gold . . . *or do we?* Is my adoration fixed on items made of chrome and silver? Where is it that I am focusing most of my time? A sport? A hobby? A possession? Oh, I hope not. But I take Jeremiah's counsel seriously, "*Consider ye . . .*" (Jeremiah 9:17; emphasis added).

Am I willing to be more like Lehi and let my possessions become of lesser consequence and the spirituality of my family become of greatest importance? Is there a way to live in the world but not be of the world? Can I learn from Lehi and Jeremiah what it will require of me to not walk the path Israel chose?

When Jeremiah asks, "Why do we sit still?" (Jeremiah 8:14), I can't help but wonder if I sit still instead of determining a plan for protecting my family. The Jerusalem Nephi grew up in was described by Jeremiah as being sensual and materialistic, and Lehi decided he couldn't afford to sit still and let that environment destroy his children. I can't help but think of our world today. Do we allow wickedness to surround us through conversations, through media, through daily life, and do we just sit still? Or do we assemble our family with a plan of defense? Do we follow the counsel of the prophets, like the call from the prophet Jeremiah to his people, "To whom shall I speak, and give warning? . . . I am weary with holding in" (Jeremiah 6:10–11). I want to hear the warnings from the prophet. I want to choose righteousness. I want to walk the path that will allow me to know the Lord. To really know Him. To understand Him.

Instead of choosing a god that can't move, speak, or go, I want to choose the living God. The One who delights in lovingkindness . . . the God who is able to do good. So, I will learn from Lehi and Jeremiah. I will listen to the prophet. My possessions matter least. My family matters most. I choose the Lord—to worship Him. I will not sit still. —EBF

Reflect and Respond

How could you be better at protecting your home and your family?

Your favorite scripture in Jeremiah 8

JEREMIAH 17:7

**Blessed is the man that trusteth in the Lord,
and whose hope the Lord is.**

Many years ago, I went on a river hike. At the very beginning of the hike, my nephew, Camden, said to me, "Oh, Em, I have to show you my favorite tree. You're just gonna love this tree." "What am I going to love about it?" I asked him. "You're just gonna love it," he replied. So, we hiked—him running ahead and then turning around to wait. We walked through the river, up the trails, over rocks, and I just kept watching for *the tree.*

I wasn't sure how he would know we had reached the tree. We had passed hundreds of trees already, and I could see more in front of us. They lined the entire riverbed, trees of all different kinds, shapes, and sizes. *What is it,* I wondered, *that sets his tree apart from the others?*

Then we came around a bend, and without him even having to say a word, I knew we had reached *the tree.* And he was right—I loved it. I am not sure why I loved it so much, but I did. Immediately. Perhaps it was the shade it provided across the entire path. It might have been the rocks that seemed strategically placed by nature herself right at the trunk to offer a spot of rest and refuge from the heat. It could have been the low boughs that stretched across the path on one side and over the river on the other. Strong boughs, just right for climbing in. Boughs that had a large curve every so often along the branch, almost as if the tree had prepared a sitting place for those who chose to venture there. It was the largest tree along the riverbank. The trunk was old and weathered. The tallest branches reached high above the other trees that lined the path. As I stood there, sheltered by its shade, I couldn't help but wonder what stories it could tell of others who had stood beneath its sheltering boughs.

Jeremiah spoke of a man whose heart had departed from the Lord, a person who would rather trust in another man than in God. He likened this man to a juniper tree growing in "the desert . . . the parched places . . . the wilderness" (Jeremiah 17:5–6). Then he spoke of a man that trusted in the Lord, and whose hope the Lord is. "He shall be as a tree planted by the waters, and that spreadeth out her roots by the river, and shall not see when heat cometh, but her leaf shall be green; and shall not be careful in the year of drought, neither shall cease from yielding fruit" (Jeremiah 17:8). I love the thought of the Lord offering refuge from heat, faith in time of drought, and fruit in every season. My thoughts turn to the blessings of protection, guidance, sustenance . . . and then, to hope.

Someday perhaps I will grow old and weathered, with roots spreading and branches reaching. Maybe a young boy will say of me, "I have to show you one of my favorite people; you will love her." "What am I going to love about her?" the person might ask. He will reply, "You're just going to love her." And when they come around the bend and see me standing there, perhaps they will recognize me as the person the boy was speaking of and think to themselves, "Oh, I *do* love her." And they may not know why, exactly, but I hope they will see in me the kind of person whose hope the Lord is. —EBF

Reflect and Respond

Why is the Lord your hope?

Your favorite
scripture in
Jeremiah 17

JEREMIAH 24:7

**I will be their God: for they shall return
unto me with their whole heart.**

Have you ever told someone, "I'm doing this for your own good . . ."? I think I remember my mom saying that once when I got my mouth washed out with soap. I totally deserved it. I said something I shouldn't have (which I won't write down here because some moments are better kept vague). It seems like those words, *for your good,* are the introduction to a consequence you are about to receive for a choice you made and now regret. These chapters in Jeremiah talk about a moment like that. The verses remind us that every choice has a consequence. If you make a good choice, then the consequence is good. But if the choice is bad, then so is the consequence. You can't escape a consequence. That is what the Lord tried to explain in chapter 21 of Jeremiah.

Once the people realized that they were about to receive a consequence they didn't want, they thought that they would look to the Lord after all. They decided to try to escape the consequence by glossing over their mistake. But it doesn't work like that. The consequence that resulted from their choice was coming regardless—they could choose to fight against it, or they could surrender to the consequence of the choice they had made, learn from the mistake, and repent.

The Lord told them, "Behold, I set before you the way of life, and the way of death. He that abideth in this city shall die by the sword, and by the famine, and by the pestilence: but he that goeth out, and falleth [surrenders] to the Chaldeans that besiege you, he shall live" (Jeremiah 21:8–9).

The Chaldeans were coming either way. They could fight against the consequence and die by the sword, or they could surrender to the consequence, learn from it through humility, and live.

The Lord gave a promise to those who were willing to accept the consequence and learn from it. I will "acknowledge them that are carried away captive of Judah, whom I have sent out of this place into the land of the Chaldeans *for their good.* For I will set mine eyes upon them *for good,* and I will bring them again to this land: and I will build them, and not pull them down, and I will plant them, and not pluck them up. And I will give them an heart to know me, that I am the Lord: and they shall be my people, and I will be their God: for they shall return unto me with their whole heart" (Jeremiah 24:5–7; emphasis added).

There are so many powerful lessons about repentance contained within those three verses. First, the Lord teaches that a consequence is often meant *for our good.* It is our choice to fight against it or to learn from it. Second, if we are humble and willing to surrender to the lesson we are given, the experience can build us and help us to grow. Third, true repentance can turn our hearts to the Lord. Through the process, we come to know Him. That knowledge leads us to understand that He is our Savior in a way we might not otherwise have learned. For repentance to be complete, we must return to the Lord with our whole heart. Not just a part of it, the whole of it. —EBF

Reflect and Respond

What is the greatest lesson you have learned through repentance?

Your favorite scripture in
Jeremiah 24

JEREMIAH 29:11

**. . . thoughts of peace, and not of evil,
to give you an expected end.**

Near my house, there is a huge field that sits vacant all through the year. No one plants on it. No one waters it. Most of the time it is covered in dry weeds and baked mud. Except for today. Today it was completely covered in beautiful yellow flowers. As I drove by, I thought, *Can beauty be found in wilderness places?* Which led me to wonder, *Can contentment be found in captivity? Can peace be found in the midst of great trial?*

In this part of Jeremiah we read of a group of people who have not found favor with the Lord. Because of their disobedience, the Lord allowed them to be carried away captive from Jerusalem into Babylon. Sometimes our refining moments come as a result of our own choices. Other times they come through the process of mortality, by no choice or consequence of our own making. Either way, the lesson we are about to learn from Jeremiah is applicable.

As the people enter into captivity, the Lord counsels them, "Build ye houses, and dwell in them; and plant gardens, and eat the fruit of them; take ye wives, and beget sons and daughters; and take wives for your sons, and give your daughters to husbands, that they may bear sons and daughters; *that ye may be increased there, and not diminished*" (Jeremiah 29:5–6; emphasis added). Obviously, these people are about to spend a lot of time in that captivity, that place of refinement—enough time to build houses, plant gardens, marry, and raise children and grandchildren. This news must have been worrisome to the people, for immediately they knew this refinement process wasn't going to just last a couple of years, it was going to be decades. They would have to wait on the Lord, which meant they would have to trust His timing.

The Lord gave them some important counsel—through that period of trial He wanted them to experience an increase and not be diminished. Is the same lesson applicable in our own lives? Can we experience growth through trial? Can we experience an increase?

Then the Lord said, "Seek the peace of the city whither I have caused you to be carried away captives, and pray unto the Lord for it: for in the peace thereof shall ye have peace"

(Jeremiah 29:7). The footnote for *peace* shows the Greek translation of the word as *contentment*. I find it interesting that the Lord counseled the people to find contentment in the place of captivity. It is difficult to be content with the place where you are when it's not the place where you want to be.

The last counsel the Lord gave Jeremiah's people included a blessing: "After seventy years be accomplished at Babylon I will visit you, and perform my good word toward you, in causing you to return to this place. *For I know the thoughts that I think toward you,* saith the Lord, thoughts of peace . . . *to give you an expected end.* . . . And ye shall seek me, and find me, when ye shall search for me with *all* your heart. And I will be found of you" (Jeremiah 29:10–14; emphasis added).

Seventy years is a long time. The people were far from home, held captive by an unfamiliar people. But the Lord did not leave them without hope—He gave them a wonderful promise: that they would not be forgotten. He would keep them in His thoughts. He promised to send peace, to answer their prayers, and to always be found by them. There was only one condition on their part—they had to seek for Him with all their heart. One of my favorite lines in this verse is found in a footnote. "For I know the thoughts that I think toward you, . . . thoughts of peace . . . to give you an expected end" (Jeremiah 29:11). If you follow the footnote for *end,* it leads to Jeremiah 31:17, which reads, "and there is hope in thine end." —EBF

Reflect and Respond

Are you in a place of captivity? How could you find contentment in knowing there is hope?

Your favorite scripture in Jeremiah 29

JEREMIAH 42:10-12

**I will plant you . . . for I am with you . . . and
I will shew mercies unto you.**

Do you have a favorite? My mother will tell you that I have a lot of favorites. Every song is my favorite song, every holiday is my favorite holiday, every scripture is my favorite scripture. I am that kind of person. I really, really love a lot of things.

I also have a favorite flower, one I love over and above any other flower. I have planted this flower in several places in my yard, simply because I love it so much. But it only blooms once a year, and the blooms only last for a short time. Springtime finds me out watching the progress of the plants daily. From the moment the first hint of green escapes from brown dirt until heavy buds hang on spindly stems, the anticipation begins filling my heart. Toward the end, Greg and I watch the progress daily, waiting for the delicate petals to burst from the tight round balls that contain them. Then I carefully cut the stems so I can bring the blossoms into my home.

I have a special crystal cut-glass vase that was my grandmother's. It is reserved specifically for these, my most favorite flowers. The blossoms will travel room to room with me for as long as they are blooming over the next several weeks. When I am cooking, they are in the kitchen windowsill. When I am writing, they are there next to me on the desk. Every evening I carry them into my bedroom and set them carefully on my nightstand next to my bed. When I breathe deep, the soft, sweet fragrance fills me up all the way into the depths of my heart.

If you were to ask me why I love these flowers so much, I think this would be my reply—they keep back nothing. Spring brings with it the promise of their coming. Their delicate petals bursting from seemingly unyielding constraints never cease to delight me. And their fragrance can fill an entire room with a penetrating softness that somehow reaches right into my heart. Perhaps it is because these flowers are so hard to come by. Maybe it's the fact that they can't be purchased from the corner grocery store. Could it be the waiting that makes me love the flowers so much? Because every year it is the same. My heart waits for springtime and the promise that the peonies will bloom again.

I wonder if the same can be said about the promises of the Lord. The tender-mercy moments often come after the waiting, from seemingly unyielding constraints. Penetrating, one-on-one moments with the Lord somehow reach right down into the depths of our heart.

Jeremiah speaks of a time like this. After the people have pled to know what the Lord would have them do, in the moment of confinement, before the blessings, Jeremiah the prophet replied, "I have heard you; behold, I will pray unto the Lord your God according to your words; and it shall come to pass, that whatsoever thing the Lord shall answer you, I will declare it unto you; I will keep nothing back from you" (Jeremiah 42:4). I will keep nothing back. "And [he] said unto them, Thus saith the Lord, the God of Israel . . . *If ye will still abide* in this land, then will I build you . . . and I will plant you. . . . Be not afraid . . . for I am with you to save you . . . and I will shew mercies unto you" (Jeremiah 42:9–12; emphasis added). If ye will still abide. "I will perform that good thing which I have promised" (Jeremiah 33:14).

I am reminded of the peonies that will abide with me in every room, wherever I go in those few weeks of spring. So it is with the Lord. There will be moments of waiting. There will be times when all that we hope for seems bound by unyielding constraints. Sometimes it may feel as if the blessings are few and far between. But ours is a Lord of tender mercies. He will perform that good thing which He has promised.

He will keep nothing back. —EBF

Reflect and Respond
When has the Lord kept nothing back from you?

Your favorite scripture in
Jeremiah 42

JEREMIAH 44:15

. . . and all the women that stood by . . .

"Then all the men which knew that their wives had burned incense unto other gods, *and all the women that stood by*, a great multitude . . . answered Jeremiah, saying, As for the word that thou hast spoken unto us in the name of the Lord, we will not hearken unto thee. But we will certainly do whatsoever thing goeth forth out of our own mouth" (Jeremiah 44:15–17; emphasis added). I was caught off guard by the second phrase in that verse, *all the women that stood by*. It struck me deeply that the women who simply stood by and watched were as wrong as the women who had chosen to worship other gods. It made me think about times in my life when I have stood by.

In my thinking, I realized that the action of standing by can take place for both good and bad. In the case of the days of Jeremiah, the women who stood by and watched the worship of other gods had made a choice that would affect their future negatively. But then I found this quote from President Gordon B. Hinckley, who spoke of the good and faithful servants who have carried forward this work from the beginning. "They were present in the home of Peter Whitmer when the Church was organized. They were among *the few who stood by the Prophet* in the troubled days of the New York period of the Church. They readily left Kirtland to serve missions wherever they were asked to go, at the call of the Prophet. . . . *They stood by the Prophet* in Liberty Jail. Peeled and driven, they staggered with the destitute Saints across the bottomlands of the Mississippi and into Quincy, Illinois.

"They drained the swamps of Commerce to create Nauvoo the Beautiful. They erected the magnificent house of the Lord on the hill above the river. . . . With mobs at their backs they abandoned their homes and temple and faced the Iowa winter. Some of them marched the long, long road with the Mormon Battalion to San Diego and then back to the valley of the Great Salt Lake. . . . Through all of this long odyssey there were those who were not loyal, some few who were traitors, who were betrayers, but they were a small minority. *Honor be to those who stood firm*, and to their wives who worked beside them."[24]

There is an important lesson here.

In the chapters that follow these scriptural verses, Jeremiah recounts the devastation that follows the army of Babylon—the destruction he had prophesied about. In that moment, each of those women who stood by learned an important lesson: Jeremiah was, in fact, a prophet. All along he had been speaking for the Lord. By the time the armies of Babylon approached, it was too late to decide that Jeremiah was the prophet of the Lord. Why didn't they listen sooner? Instead of being women who stood by as other wives burned incense unto other gods, why didn't they choose to stand by the prophet? To stand firm.

We, too, are part of the great odyssey President Hinckley spoke of. We are surrounded by those who are not loyal. All the days of my life, I want to be known as one of the few who stood by the prophet.

Honor be to those who stood firm. —EBF

Reflect and Respond

What can you do to stand firm in your belief?

Your favorite scripture in
Jeremiah 44

JEREMIAH 51:11-12

**Make bright the arrows;
gather the shields. . . . Set up the standard.**

It is not hard to visualize the preparation taking place for the battle at hand: shields being gathered, standards set up along the walls, watchtowers strengthened and manned. But it is the idea of making the arrows bright that catches my attention. It makes me think that just gathering the arrows was not enough—there was work to be done in making sure the arrows were ready for the battle. They had to be made bright. Perhaps it was the responsibility of the holder of the bow to make sure his arrows were prepared.

Then I read this quote from Elder Jeffrey R. Holland, and suddenly the lesson turned from physical arrows used in warfare to spiritual arrows and the battles that rage in the hearts of men today: "We anxiously watch that arrow in flight and know all the evils that can deflect its course after it has left our hand, nevertheless we take courage in remembering that the most important mortal factor in determining that arrow's destination will be the stability, strength, and unwavering certainty of the holder of the bow."[25]

We are the holder of the bow. Where does our stability come from? Where do we turn for strength? In what areas is our certainty unwavering? Perhaps we should pause to consider, because if the most important factor in determining the destination of our arrow rests upon those three things, then the answers to those questions become crucial. Within those answers there is something to be discovered—what lies beneath the stability, the strength, and the certainty is the very essence of what we believe. As President James E. Faust said, "Your own personal testimony is the strongest arrow in your quiver."[26] —EBF

Reflect and Respond

Where do your stability, strength, and unwavering certainty come from?

Your favorite scripture in Jeremiah 51

LAMENTATIONS 3:22-23

His compassions fail not.
They are new every morning.

Most mornings I go for a walk. It gives me time to think. When things aren't going particularly well, I like to walk by myself. On those mornings I walk and I pray. It never seems to fail, once my soul gets in its humble place, my eyes become open. I see things I might not have noticed before.

Every new morning it is the same. It begins as I notice His beauty surrounding me—I hear the brook flowing and the birds chirping. I feel the breeze on my face and the warmth of the sun on my shoulders. Then, somewhere within, my heart begins to swell with the gratitude. There, within the gratitude, comes the whisper of a great truth—if He is the creator of all this goodness and the designer of all that surrounds, if He gave attention to the detail of the smallest white blossom and added a brilliant yellow flower to the top of what most would consider a simple weed, if He shaped trees whose giant boughs would offer shade from intense heat and grasses that would whisper gently in the wind, *then what might He do with my life?*

Through His compassion and His mercy, might He take this soul that longs for peace and prosperity, that yearns for strength and hope, that cries within from affliction and sometimes even misery, and make it something more? Could He give attention to the small details and add brilliance to the parts that seem too simple? Might He offer refuge from the intensity? Could He whisper gentle words of inspiration along the way? Would I become new? "This I recall to my mind, therefore have I hope. It is of the Lord's mercies that we are not consumed, because his compassions fail not. They are new every morning" (Lamentations 3:21–23). —EBF

Reflect and Respond

How have you experienced the Lord's compassion?

Your favorite scripture in **Lamentations 3**

EZEKIEL 2:5

There hath been a prophet among them.

In my dad's study hangs a framed quote by President Thomas S. Monson. There is nothing really amazing about the presentation. It's typed on a white piece of paper. The matting is not remarkable. It's not much to look at, but my dad treasures it. President Thomas S. Monson gave that piece of paper to my dad a long time ago, after a conversation they had shared. Scribbled across the top in simple ballpoint pen is an endearing note, "To my Dear Friend Mac" and at the bottom is a signature, "Thomas S. Monson."

Here is what I love about that framed quote: every time I look at it, I am reminded of an important truth—my dad was a friend to the prophet. They were not friends in the sense that they spoke often or spent a lot of time with each other. They were friends in the fact that they both supported a common cause. They were builders in the kingdom.

Consider this verse from Ezekiel, "I do send thee unto them; and thou shalt say unto them, Thus saith the Lord God. And they, whether they will hear, or whether they will forbear, (for they are a rebellious house,) *yet shall know that there hath been a prophet among them*" (Ezekiel 2:4–5; emphasis added). Ezekiel's people knew that there was a prophet of God right in their midst—a prophet whose sole responsibility was to teach the words of the Lord. Yet some would choose not to hear him. It makes my heart sad. After reading that verse, I make a decision. I want to be a little more like my dad. I want to be a friend to the prophet. Always. —EBF

Reflect and Respond

How could you show that you are a friend to the prophet?

Your favorite scripture in Ezekiel 2

EZEKIEL 13:11

Say unto them which daub it with
untempered mortar, that it shall fall.

Some time ago I went for a walk with my husband in Cancun, Mexico. We came upon the most interesting wall I have ever seen. It was not a beautiful wall. The structure was made out of tan cinderblocks held together with grey mortar. The mortar job was one of the messiest I have ever seen. The grey cement was not confined to its place in between the blocks but dripped all the way down the side of the wall. Across the top of the wall someone had placed shards of broken glass and mirrors in the mortar before it dried to dissuade anyone from climbing over.

Reading Ezekiel reminded me of the wall: "And one built up a wall, and, lo, others daubed it with untempered mortar: Say unto them which daub it with untempered mortar, that it shall fall. . . . Lo, when the wall is fallen, shall it not be said unto you, Where is the daubing wherewith ye have daubed it?" (Ezekiel 13:10–12).

It makes you wonder, *what was the untempered mortar, the daubing?* Ezekiel 22:28 gives us a hint: "And her prophets have daubed them with untempered mortar, seeing vanity, and divining lies unto them, saying, Thus saith the Lord God, when the Lord hath not spoken."

The untempered mortar came from false prophets who spoke lies, who were filled with self-absorption and pride, who said they were speaking for God. They were not. A wall built with this type of mortar cannot stand. It lacks strength. It is messy. It is built to dissuade.

I contrast that with the words of holy prophets—those who speak to us today and those who have gone before. I consider how their words fill up these pages of scripture.

Their words are becoming our mortar. They will be our strength. —EBF

Reflect and Respond
How are you strengthening your mortar?

Your favorite scripture in **Ezekiel 13**

EZEKIEL 22:30

**And I sought for a man ... that should ... stand
in the gap ... but I found none.**

In the book of Ezekiel, the Lord speaks of the great battle of the last days. He is worried that the Saints will not prepare themselves sufficiently to be protected. "Ye have not gone up into the gaps, neither made up the hedge for the house of Israel to stand in the battle in the day of the Lord" (Ezekiel 13:5). Where there were gaps in the hedge, there would be a lack of protection, and the enemy could enter in. In order to compensate for the gaps, Ezekiel "sought for a man among them, that should make up the hedge, and stand in the gap before ... the land ... *but I found none*" (Ezekiel 22:30; emphasis added).

This scripture haunts me—why could he not find a man to stand in the gap? Was there no one to offer strength against the enemy in the places where the hedge didn't offer enough protection?

We live in the era Ezekiel prophesied of. The battle rages fiercely around us, and if we look carefully, we might be able to detect the gaps in the hedge. Someone needs to fill the gaps. Someone needs to make up the hedge.

What would we have to do to qualify ourselves for that position? What is it that we need to do so that we can be ready and prepared? What will help us to be found of the Lord in the moment when He needs us most? The book of Ezekiel lists the things that *won't* qualify us to stand in the gap:

- follow foolish prophets
- take counsel from those who speak lies, and see vanity
- use oppression, persecution, cruelty
- exercise robbery or deception
- vex the poor and needy
- oppress the stranger wrongfully

Perhaps if we look at the opposite of these characteristics from the list above, we might find clues as to what we *should* do:

- follow the prophet
- take counsel from those who speak the truth
- let our first response be kindness
- live with integrity
- serve, reach out, assist

It is an interesting set of requirements. I find myself questioning, *are these qualities characteristic of a warrior?* At first glance, they do not seem like the qualifications I would expect for someone who would be prepared to stand in a battle, to make up the hedge, or even to go up into the gaps. It makes me realize that we might not fully understand the nature of the battle that rages around us. If our strength is to be found through obtaining counsel and learning kindness, integrity, and charity, then we won't have to look far. Our best resource for the most recent counsel pertaining to the war that rages around us is easy to obtain. From the words of the prophets we can learn about all the qualities that will help us to become the type of people qualified to make up the hedge and to stand in the gaps. It isn't hard to immerse ourselves in the counsel that will offer our families the strength we need—so that we can be found of the Lord. —EBF

Reflect and Respond

How can you prepare to make up the hedge and stand in the gap?

Your favorite scripture in Ezekiel 22

EZEKIEL 34:11

I, even I, will both search my sheep, and seek them out.

On this occasion, Ezekiel is reproving the shepherds who do not feed the flocks. "Thus saith the Lord God . . . should not the shepherds feed the flocks? . . . The diseased have ye not strengthened, neither have ye healed that which was sick, neither have ye bound up that which was broken, neither have ye brought again that which was driven away, neither have ye sought that which was lost . . . and they were scattered, because there is no shepherd" (Ezekiel 34:2, 4–5).

My heart hurts for the sick one that was not healed, the broken one that was not bound up, the one that was not strengthened, the lost one, and the one that was driven away.

Why was there no one to care for them?

My sister raises sheep. Once, one of the ewes delivered three baby lambs. Finding it too hard to care for all three babies, the mother began to neglect the smallest lamb. My sister was aware that this might happen. She had been watching over her flock. So, even though it would require sacrifice, she decided to mother this little lamb. She made a makeshift bed for it in her kitchen, and she let it follow her all through her house. The little lamb's favorite place to be was right under my sister's feet. It felt safe there. Watched over. Cared for.

My sister named that little lamb Joy. It makes me happy that the one who was broken and driven away and uncared for was given such a happy name.

The experience of watching my sister care for her little lamb made my heart tender toward the way this chapter in Ezekiel ends. After expressing His unhappiness with the shepherds of Israel, the Lord extended a beautiful promise, "For thus saith the Lord God; Behold, I, even I, will both search my sheep, and seek them out. As a shepherd seeketh out his flock in the day that he is among his sheep . . . so will I seek out my sheep, and will deliver them out of all places where they have been scattered in the cloudy and dark day . . . and feed them upon the mountains of Israel by the rivers. . . . I will feed them in a good pasture . . . there shall they lie in a good fold. . . . *I will seek that which was lost, and bring again that which was driven away, and will bind up that which was broken, and will strengthen that which was sick.* . . . And I will make them and the places round about my hill a blessing; and I will cause the shower to come down in his season; there shall be showers of blessing. . . . Thus shall they know that I the Lord their God am with them" (Ezekiel 34:11–16, 26, 30; emphasis added).

There is One who is watching over us on our cloudy and dark days. He will seek us when we are lost, bring us back when we are driven away, bind us up when we are broken, and give us strength beyond our own. We are His joy, upon whom He will send showers of blessing. —EBF

Reflect and Respond

How has He searched you out? What did you learn from that experience?

Your favorite scripture in **Ezekiel 34**

EZEKIEL 47:9

**Every thing . . . whithersoever the
rivers shall come, shall live.**

There is so much to learn from the vision in which a heavenly ministrant shows Ezekiel the temple. I love his opening counsel: "Set thine heart upon all that I shall shew thee" (Ezekiel 40:4). Ezekiel talks about walking through the waters that issue out from under the threshold of the house, "and he brought me through the waters; the waters were to the ankles . . . and brought me through the waters; the waters were to the knees . . . and brought me through; the waters were to the loins . . . and it was a river that I could not pass over: for the waters were risen, waters to swim in, *a river that could not be passed over*" (Ezekiel 47:3–5; emphasis added).

As I read, my thoughts fill with memories of moments I have spent in the temple when my heart has been so broken that just stepping in up to my ankles is not sufficient. The times I remember most are those when I have fully immersed myself in that holy, sacred place. The sanctuary of refuge and safety for my heart. As I have turned my heart to Christ in that place, the healing has come. Blessings can be found within: poured out, spilling over, overflowing.

Toward the end of Ezekiel's vision of the temple, just after the lesson of fully being immersed in the water, an interesting thing happens: the living waters fill the temple and spill out of the east side of the holy place and flow down to the Dead Sea. If you have ever been to the Dead Sea, you realize how remarkable that is. The surrounding area is lifeless desert. It is dry. It is hot. It is miserable. The Dead Sea supports no life. The salt content is so high it allows nothing to grow or thrive. The waters burn the smallest paper cut on your skin; they are disgusting to the taste and almost unbearable if even a drop gets in your eye. The sea may look refreshing against the sand dunes, but it is deceiving. In addition to all of this, it also happens to be the lowest spot of land on the whole earth, and it is lowering with each passing year. It is not only dead, it is continually dying. You cannot find a more lifeless and helpless spot on earth.

But Ezekiel speaks of a remarkable promise: "These waters issue out toward the east country, and go down into the desert, and go into the sea: which being brought forth into the sea, *the waters shall be healed.* And it shall come to pass, that every thing . . . whithersoever the rivers shall come, *shall live:* and there shall be a very great multitude of fish, because these waters shall come thither: for *they shall be healed;* and *every thing shall live whither the river cometh*" (Ezekiel 47:8–9; emphasis added).

The waters that flow from the temple will heal the Dead Sea, and "every thing shall live."

That is perhaps one of the most unbelievable lessons in the Old Testament. The common eye would see water that is not healable. But those who remember to separate the common from the sacred, to see the holy, will understand that the waters from the temple are symbolic of the healing power of Jesus Christ. They flow from the temple—the sanctuary, the place of healing.

A place where we can be completely immersed in healing, mercy, and grace. And the healing waters seem to find the spots that need them most.

The Atonement of Christ can heal anyone, anything, anytime. If these waters can heal the lowest, driest, darkest, most disgusting place on earth, then there is not a soul on that earth that is out of reach of the flowing, healing power of Jesus. You can set your heart on that promise.

I do believe those waters will one day flow from the source and touch every part of God's earth. But I also believe we can immerse ourselves in them now. In places of covenants. In places of mercy. In places of peace. In places of God. His holy places. —EBF

Reflect and Respond

How have you found healing in covenant places?

Your favorite scripture in Ezekiel 47

DANIEL 3:18

**But if not, be it known unto thee, O king,
that we will not serve thy gods . . .**

When King Nebuchadnezzar established a new law in the land that required the citizens of Babylon to bow down and worship the golden image he set up, Daniel's faithful friends refused to turn their back on their God. In his rage, the king called in and questioned the three Hebrew boys. He demanded that they bow down to his idols or face immediate death in his furnaces. One of them voiced the expression of all three hearts, "O Nebuchadnezzar, we are not careful to answer thee in this matter. If it be so, our God whom we serve is able to deliver us from the burning fiery furnace, and he will deliver us out of thine hand, O king. *But if not,* be it known unto thee, O king, that we will not serve thy gods, nor worship the golden image which thou hast set up" (Daniel 3:16–18; emphasis added).

This has to be one of the most courageous statements in all of scripture. With boldness, they told the king and anyone else listening that they knew that God *could* deliver them from the fire. He could do anything He wanted to—and maybe He would. *But if not*—if His will was to let them face death—they still would not worship the gods of Nebuchadnezzar. The Lord allowed the king to attempt to force these valiant youth into certain death. In this case, they were not immediately delivered from a literal refiner's fire.

Several years ago, I found myself in the lowest days of my life so far. I hit rock bottom physically, mentally, emotionally, and spiritually. I realize that there are others who have had it worse than I did, and sometimes I feel foolish to say what trial constitutes my hardest days, but all comparisons set aside, I really experienced some dark, sad moments. A refiner's fire. There is reason to believe that God does, in fact, have the ability and desire to deliver us from the pain these moments might cause. He is the Creator of worlds without number. The great God of heaven who could have delivered Shadrach, Meshach, and Abed-nego from the fire could also deliver you and me from heartache, trouble, despair, or any of life's other tests of faith. But that isn't always what takes place in the story.

The message from these great young men is that God might have the ability to deliver us from affliction, "but if not," we must still trust Him.

One of the most powerful moments in this episode happened when the boys were in the midst of the fires. After being thrust in, each boy fell down into the scalding ash—I wonder if they were kneeling? "Then Nebuchadnezzar the king was astonished, and rose up in haste, and spake, and said unto his counsellors, Did not we cast three men bound into the midst of the fire? They answered and said unto the king, True, O king. He answered and said, Lo, I see four men loose, walking in the midst of the fire, and they have no hurt; and the form of the fourth is like the Son of God" (Daniel 3:24–25).

The story of these three boys stands as an everlasting testimony that the Savior will stand by those who stand true to Him—always. In every trial. He was not involved in this story as a heavenly spectator, but rather as a participant. I love how this account so clearly teaches the loving truth that in the middle of the burning tests of life, there is a fourth man walking in the midst of the fire. Perhaps each of us experiences the refiner's fire for just one reason—to come to *know* the Refiner and, through the proving process, to understand that Christ is always there. In the darkest hours of the night and the longest hours of the day, He is there. In the hours of suffering, perhaps the greatest comfort comes in the realization that we are not alone. Christ has said, "Ye may know of a surety that I, the Lord God, do visit my people in their afflictions" (Mosiah 24:14). —DB

Reflect and Respond

When has the Lord stood by you in a refining moment? What did you learn?

Your favorite scripture in Daniel 3

DANIEL 5:27

**Thou art weighed in the balances,
and art found wanting.**

I once had the opportunity to spend some time backstage at a theatre that was unlike any I have visited before. The walls backstage were made of red bricks that rose from floor to ceiling and spanned from left to right as far as the eye could see. Written on each individual brick was the name of a person who had performed on that stage, the year that they performed there, and a short message. I found myself captivated by them. I couldn't help but wonder what message I would have left as writing on the wall.

In the book of Daniel, Belshazzar the king had a great feast. He did not have a humble heart. He had lifted himself up against the Lord. On this particular evening, he had poured wine for his guests into the vessels that had been stolen out of the house of the Lord. In the midst of this great feast a hand sent from God left writing on the wall, "MENE, MENE, TEKEL, UPHARSIN" (Daniel 5:25). A simple translation would read, "Numbered. Numbered. Weighed. Divided."

The king felt that there was more behind the message than just those three words. He sent for his wise men, but none could translate. So, the queen suggested he call for Daniel. I love how she described him: "There is a man in thy kingdom, in whom is the spirit of the holy gods: and in the days of thy father light and understanding and wisdom, like the wisdom of the gods, was found in him" (Daniel 5:11).

So, Daniel was brought before the king. The first thing the king asked him was, "Art thou that Daniel . . . *I have even heard of thee,* that the spirit of the gods is in thee, and that light and understanding and excellent wisdom is found in thee. . . . *I have heard of thee,* that thou canst make interpretations, and dissolve doubts" (Daniel 5:13–16; emphasis added). Daniel agreed to make known the interpretation of the event to the king. He spoke of the king's father, Nebuchadnezzar, and his weaknesses and his strengths. Then he spoke of King Belshazzar, and his mistakes and the places where he was lacking in righteousness.

He spoke with the Spirit of God. He spoke wisdom and brought light and understanding. He spoke hard sentences. He spoke knowledge. And then, dissolving doubt, he interpreted the meaning of the writing. Each of the three words written on the wall had a different interpretation, but it is the middle word that catches my full attention: "TEKEL; Thou art weighed in the balances, and art found wanting" (Daniel 5:27).

There is an important lesson contained within this chapter—if you look carefully, you will see that two men were weighed in the balance. One was known for his drinking, his praise for the gods of gold, his prideful heart—he was known as a man who did not glorify God. The other was known for his excellent spirit, his light and understanding, his wisdom, his knowledge, his ability to shew hard sentences and dissolve doubt. Both were weighed in the balances, but only one was found wanting.

I love the six words King Belshazzar said of Daniel, "I have even heard of thee . . ." I can't help but think, if people were to begin a sentence, "Oh, I have heard of you . . ." how would they describe me? When weighed in the balances, would words such as those used to describe Daniel come to mind? What would I have to change in my life so that those were the words that would describe me? There will come a day when the Lord will measure me; I hope I will not be found wanting. —EBF

Reflect and Respond

Have you ever felt weighed in the balances? What was found wanting?

Your favorite scripture in Daniel 5

HOSEA 2:19

**I will betroth thee unto me in righteousness . . .
in lovingkindness, and in mercies.**

The Lord commanded Hosea the prophet to marry a woman named Gomer who had a bad reputation and a questionable past. He did what the Lord asked and married her and loved her well. Gomer, however, did not return the love. One day, Hosea came home to find Gomer gone. And she didn't just leave—she left him for someone else. She cheated on him and went back to her old, scandalous ways of life. "I will go after my lovers," she said (Hosea 2:5). Hosea was rejected and betrayed. Instead of abandoning her, like it may seem he should have, he tried to win her back to his love. "I will allure her," he said (Hosea 2:14). Tragically, Gomer had been sold into slavery for some of the choices she made. In a surprising move, Hosea went after her and finally found her, broken and enslaved. Then, he bought her back from the slave owners!

Hosea does not seem to be writing the book to give marriage or relationship advice, but to give a metaphor. A metaphor of the love story between the Lord and Israel. Hosea is the Lord, and Israel is Gomer. The Lord had been so good to Israel and had loved Israel despite their choices. Israel cheated on Him with sin. They turned their back and left him for the worship of other gods. But He still reached out to them, the same way Hosea did to Gomer.

I have gone off in my own way to find other things that make me happy. There have been plenty of times when I have ignored His constant and kind requests and then gotten myself deep in trouble and debt and slavery, but He buys me back and allures me with His loving and tender kindness time and time again. To be loved so undeservedly is heaven. —DB

Reflect and Respond

When has God shown you undeserved affection and love?

Your favorite
scripture in
Hosea

JOEL 2:28

And it shall come to pass afterward,
that **I will pour out my spirit upon all flesh**.

It is difficult to know in what time period Joel lived and performed his ministry, but his book of scripture is filled with allusions to other books of scripture. Some of those recount great moments in history when God performed His wonders among His people. In addition to the marvelous acts of the past, Joel prophesied about similar amazing things happening in the future as well. One of his prophecies was one that Moroni quoted to Joseph Smith the night he first visited him in his bedroom. Moroni quoted several Old Testament passages, including at least one from the book of Joel: "And it shall come to pass afterward, that I will pour out my spirit upon all flesh; and your sons and your daughters shall prophesy, your old men shall dream dreams, your young men shall see visions" (Joel 2:28). When Moroni quoted this ancient prophesy, he told Joseph that this "was not yet fulfilled, but was soon to be" (Joseph Smith—History 1:41).

It is thrilling to me to consider the fact that you and I may live in that "soon to be" time period when God has begun and is continuing to pour out His Spirit upon all people. This is a day when we can anticipate and look forward to great things that God will be doing even among the most normal of us—our sons and daughters, our old men and young men. As a teacher of youth for the last decade and a half, I have been an eyewitness of half of that prophecy—the one about the young men and women. I have heard their dreams, I have listened to their hopeful views of the future, and I have experienced what it is like to be in close company with those who have had God's Spirit not just trickled, but poured out upon them. —DB

Reflect and Respond
When have you seen evidence of God's Spirit being poured out upon all flesh?

Your favorite scripture in
Joel

AMOS 5:24

**But let judgment run down as waters,
and righteousness as a mighty stream.**

Amos the prophet was a fig-tree farmer and a shepherd who lived on the border of the two divided kingdoms of northern Israel and southern Judah. During his days, the northern kingdom, under the leadership of Jeroboam II, was very successful in war and wealth, but was poor in true worship of God. The people of Israel had become a nation obsessed with money and selfishness and had neglected the underprivileged and poor among them. The book of Amos is a collection of the words, poems, and prophecies of this shepherd-prophet who went into the northern kingdom to speak against the way they were living.

"For thus saith the Lord unto the house of Israel, Seek ye me, and ye shall live" (Amos 5:4). The people appeared to be seeking Him, for they were offering their sacrifices in the temple, celebrating their holy days, and playing songs of worship. However, the Lord told them that He despised these actions. The outward expressions of worship were of no value to the Lord unless they flowed out of a heart that was filled with love. "Let judgment run down as waters, and righteousness as a mighty stream" (Amos 5:24). These calls of "judgment" and "righteousness" are invitations to care for people who are suffering unjustly and to reach out in relationship and kindness to others—perhaps particularly to those who are different. That is the way to seek Him best—by loving other people well. "Seek good . . . that ye may live" (Amos 5:14). Seeking God and seeking to do that which is good to others are synonyms to the Lord. He wants these to be the marks of true worship. He wants these to flow through His people like a mighty river. —DB

Reflect and Respond
When was the last time you witnessed someone worship truly by loving well?

Your favorite
scripture in
Amos

OBADIAH 1:17

**But upon mount Zion shall be deliverance,
and there shall be holiness.**

Obadiah's is the smallest book of the Old Testament, and it is hard to know who he was and what time period he lived in. Most of his short twenty-one verses were a rebuke from the Lord against the country called Edom. Edom is a nation that was next to Israel, and, according to the context clues of Obadiah, it was not a kind neighbor. The people of Edom were descendants of Esau, and the people of Israel were descendants of Jacob. Those twin brothers from the book of Genesis had a rocky relationship with each other for many years, and it seems like the animosity continued. When the nation of Judah was taken away by Babylon as exiles and the city of Jerusalem destroyed, Edom not only refused to help, but they also ransacked the city alongside the Babylonians, took over houses and possessions that were left behind, and prevented any runaways or escaped refugees from finding shelter in their lands.

The way the Edomites treated their brothers and sisters seems to be a type and shadow of the despicable actions of all of humanity against each other. There is so much unkindness, pride, and brokenness in our world that reflects what we read about in Obadiah. But his story ends with hope. He prophesied that the once-destroyed city of Jerusalem—the place where so much betrayal and atrocity took place—would one day be a place of deliverance and holiness. By the grace of God, the once-awful conditions would be turned upside down into something amazing. A story filled with allusions of brother fighting against brother is a story that ends with them not as enemies to each other, but as "saviours" on Mount Zion (Obadiah 1:21). A place now filled with self-sacrificing kindness. A place that would be called the kingdom of God. —DB

Reflect and Respond

In what ways can we be saviors on Mount Zion?

Your favorite scripture in
Obadiah

JONAH 1:6

What meanest thou, O sleeper? arise...

Jonah's story is familiar to us. The task from the Lord. The running away from Nineveh. The boat. The storm. The throwing overboard. The big fish. The three days in the belly. Every time I read it, I can't help but think about how Jonah's story in the Bible compares to Alma's story in the Book of Mormon.

Two prophets were called of God. Both were asked to cry repentance to very wicked cities—one to Nineveh, the other to Ammonihah. Persecution, discouragement, perhaps failure, and possibly even death awaited them within the city walls.

But the Lord had a purpose in mind for these two cities. He knew these men were capable of preaching the gospel with the Spirit. He knew the Spirit was capable of changing hearts.

The difference in the two accounts is the way each prophet responded to the commandment of the Lord. Jonah "rose up to flee" (Jonah 1:3). "After Alma had received his message from the angel of the Lord he *returned speedily* . . . and he entered the city by another way" (Alma 8:18; emphasis added).

In Alma's case, the Lord had prepared the way before him so that he could accomplish the great work in store. An angel had been sent; a man's heart was softened; a companion was waiting to assist in the work.

In Jonah's case, the Lord had also prepared a way for him to accomplish the great work in store. The Lord sent the wind, caused a mighty tempest, and "*prepared* a great fish to swallow up Jonah" (Jonah 1:17; emphasis added).

There is an important lesson here. The doctrine of this lesson can be found within the words of a well-known letter written by Joseph Smith. "The standard of truth has been erected: no unhallowed hand can stop the work from progressing, persecutions may rage, mobs may combine, armies may assemble, calumny may defame, but the truth of God will go forth boldly, nobly, and independent till it has penetrated every continent, visited every clime, swept every country, and sounded in every ear, till the purposes of God shall be accomplished and the Great Jehovah shall say the work is done."[27]

Nothing can stop the work of the Lord. If we act upon the direction we are given and allow the Spirit to be our guide, great blessings await us. He will prepare the way for us to accomplish His great work, even if it requires unlikely adventures.

One of my favorite lines in the story of Jonah happens just after he has fled to the ship, as the ship is being tossed by the great tempest in the sea. Jonah is fast asleep. "So the shipmaster came to him, and said unto him, What meanest thou, O sleeper? arise, call upon thy God" (Jonah 1:6).

It has caused me to analyze my own life. Are there areas in which I am sleeping as the tempest rages around me? Am I missing out on a great work I could be performing on the Lord's behalf within my family, my calling, or my circle of influence?

O sleeper? Arise . . .

He knows the great work He has in store for you. —EBF

Reflect and Respond

Are there places in your life where you are sleeping right now?

Your favorite scripture in
Jonah

MICAH 6:14

Thou shalt eat, but not be satisfied.

As I sat in the dentist chair, I felt the regret. The hard lemon candy that had seemed so appealing hadn't been worth the dull ache keeping me up at night, or the cost of now repairing the damage. The satisfaction from the sweet sugar had been momentary, the consequences lasting. And now, I sat in the dentist's chair waiting for him to fix a problem I couldn't resolve on my own. In that moment, sitting in the chair with my lip growing numb, one thought kept running through my mind: as sweet as it was, that lemon drop just hadn't been worth it.

After I left the office, I read this verse in Micah: "Thou shalt eat, but not be satisfied; and thy casting down shall be in the midst of thee" (Micah 6:14). The footnote makes it easier to understand. "Thou shalt eat, but not be satisfied; thy hunger shall be in thy inward parts." After my lemon-drop experience, I can sort of understand what it means to eat something and not be satisfied. But I don't think Micah was talking about lemon drops. I think he was talking about spiritual hunger, the kind of hunger that is down deep inside.

Sometimes we try to take care of that hunger, that longing, that aching, with that which cannot satisfy. If we are not careful, our choice might cause us pain. It might come with a cost we are not willing to pay. It might even lead to greater hunger, emptiness that reaches deep into our inward parts. The Savior knows how to satisfy our hungering, our yearning, our aching. I have felt His ability to soothe the longing in my own life. I have seen Him heal the aching in the hearts of those I love. He understands our innermost longing. He knows our wants. He knows our needs. Only He can bring that which will satisfy. Through Him, we will become full. —EBF

Reflect and Respond

How is your emptiness satisfied in the Lord?

Your favorite scripture in
Micah

NAHUM 1:7

. . . a strong hold in the day of trouble.

A friend of my daughter once went rappelling with a youth group. Some of the group stood on the top of the mountain waiting. Others watched from below. One was assigned to hold the rope at the bottom. This post was crucial. His job was to hold the end of the rope as the climber descended down the face of the cliff. His dedication to the job ensured safety for the one who was attempting the descent. In essence, the person descending was placing his very survival in the hand of the one holding the rope.

On this particular day, there were two groups rappelling. As my daughter's friend descended, he heard a boy from the other group yell from the top of the cliff that he was about to start his descent. What the boy didn't know, because he couldn't see the bottom, was that the person assigned to hold the other end of his rope had left his post. The boy jumped off the top of the cliff and fell 110 feet to the bottom. Miraculously, his life was spared. He sustained major injuries, but he lived. Sadly, the danger, the cries of fear, the excruciating pain could have all been prevented if someone had just kept a strong hold on the other end of the rope.

I love the message found in the book of Nahum: "The Lord is good, *a strong hold in the day of trouble;* and he knoweth them that trust in him" (Nahum 1:7; emphasis added). In moments of danger, fear, or pain, when it seems as if all of life is going downhill fast, we must never forget that the Lord stands waiting and watching, with a strong hold on the other end of the rope. He will not leave His post. In the day of trouble, we must put our trust in Him. He will hold on to us until we arrive safely at the end. If we rely on Him, He will not let us fall. —EBF

Reflect and Respond

How has the Lord been a strong hold in your day of trouble?

Your favorite scripture in
Nahum

HABAKKUK 2:20

But the Lord is in his holy temple.

Since the imagery of idols is a recurring theme throughout all 1184 pages of the Old Testament, I know that it must be a recurring theme now, a tradition handed down through generations. "Woe unto him that saith to the wood, Awake; to the dumb stone, Arise, it shall teach! Behold, it is laid over with gold and silver, and there is no breath at all in the midst of it. *But the Lord is in his holy temple*" (Habakkuk 2:19–21; emphasis added).

It seems ridiculous to us, I know. We cannot understand the devotion to these idols made of stone and wood and covered with gold and silver. We shake our heads. We wonder how the people could have been so ignorant. Why did they waste their time worshipping a god that had no breath at all in the midst of it? Ridiculous! But in the moments when I pray that my eyes will be open to see, I discover my own ignorance.

There is a temple less than ten minutes from my home. The Lord is in that holy temple.

And yet, my days are filled with maintaining that which I have paid for in gold and silver and built up of wood and stone. It has been said that the place where we devote most of our time is the place we worship most. It is a hard question to ask the soul: Where do I devote most of my time? Don't get me wrong, I am not suggesting that we can't have a beautiful home, that we do not need vehicles to get us where we need to go, that an honest day of work is not admirable. But today I am reminding myself that the God I worship is in His holy temple—just minutes away from my home. I know where He is. His name is there on His house. I need to balance my life in such a way that I am devoted to visiting Him there. —EBF

Reflect and Respond

How can you make spending time with the Lord a priority today?

Your favorite scripture in **Habakkuk**

ZEPHANIAH 2:1

Gather yourselves together, yea, gather together.

Every time I see a bird's nest, my thoughts become captivated with the principle of gathering. It is a painstaking process, the mother bird gathering each piece of straw, then fitting it carefully into the refuge she is building. It is becoming the place that she will visit throughout the day, and often sit in the midst of, and the babies will come, and she will rejoice over them, and the morning will be filled with their songs of joy. But first, every year, it is the same. Before the eggs can be settled within, before the babies burst out of their shells, before the constant peeping that signals new life and new hope, the process always begins with the gathering.

"Gather yourselves together, yea, gather together. . . . Before the day pass as the chaff, before the fierce anger of the Lord come upon you, . . . seek ye the Lord. . . . The Lord thy God in the midst of thee is mighty; he will save, he will rejoice over thee with joy; he will rest in his love, he will joy over thee with singing. I will gather them. . . . At that time will I bring you again, even in the time that I gather you" (Zephaniah 2:1–3; 3:17–20).

Within the building of the nest and the words of Zephaniah I learn of the doctrine of gathering. Gathering for the nest is much like the gathering of the Lord as He guides us, one by one, to find the place of refuge. A place where He will visit and be found in the midst thereof. A place where we can rejoice with joy and rest in His love. As President Henry B. Eyring said, "It is not surprising then that God urges us to gather so that He can bless us. . . . In those gatherings, which God has designed for us, lies our great opportunity. . . . We will move together in power to go wherever God would have us go and to become what He wants us to be."[28] —EBF

Reflect and Respond
How are you participating in the doctrine of gathering?

Your favorite scripture in **Zephaniah**

HAGGAI 1:7

Consider your ways.

The people of Haggai's day had become sidetracked on their journey to discipleship. They were meant to be building the temple, but they lost focus somewhere along the way. The Lord said to the people, "*Consider your ways.* Ye have sown much, and bring in little; ye eat, but ye have not enough; ye drink, but ye are not filled with drink; ye clothe you, but there is none warm; and he that earneth wages earneth wages to put it into a bag with holes. Thus saith the Lord of hosts; *Consider your ways*" (Haggai 1:5–7; emphasis added).

This description sounds a lot like our day. Our world is filled with people who work hard but bring in little, who are unsatisfied and lack a feeling of fulfillment. Unfortunately, the illustration of money slipping away is an idea that many of us can relate to. Perhaps we too should consider our ways.

The Lord explains the problem, "Ye looked for much, and, lo, it came to little . . . the heaven over you is stayed from dew, and the earth is stayed from her fruit" (Haggai 1:9–10). Somehow these people had lost focus. What accounted in their eyes as much, was in reality little. They had laid aside the most important thing—building the temple would have allowed the Lord to remain foremost in their lives. Why was that so important? Without Him, the dew from heaven and the fruit of the earth were stayed.

Dew is often used figuratively to represent inspiration from heaven. When the Lord and His house became of lesser importance to the people of Haggai, inspiration from heaven also decreased. Without inspiration from the Lord, the people were left to their own means, their own strength. The Bible Dictionary entry for "Haggai" explains that the worldly behavior of the people had brought about a curse on their labor and their increase. As unfortunate as that is, it makes sense, and we are led to wonder if the same is true in our day.

But the Lord did not forget His people.

He stirred up their spirits in remembrance, and He was forgiving. As soon as they laid the foundation for the temple, the Lord became their focus, and their lives began to change for the better. "Consider now from this day and upward . . . even from the day that the foundation of the Lord's temple was laid, consider it. Is the seed yet in the barn? yea, as yet the vine, and the fig tree, and the pomegranate, and the olive tree . . . from this day will I bless you" (Haggai 2:18–19).

Their willingness to turn to the Lord, to make Him the first priority, allowed Him to send great blessings they otherwise might not have obtained. Because their thoughts were focused on Him, they were able to receive inspiration for their lives, direction from Him that would have otherwise gone unheeded.

Is it possible that this counsel would work in our lives? What if we were to ask ourselves that same question? *Consider your ways.* Do your ways lead you to seek inspiration on a daily basis? Is the Lord a first priority? Are you asking Him for input concerning your home, your profession, and your way of life? Do you take the time to consider the blessings in your life and recognize that they come from the Lord?

Become willing to be the type of person who can answer yes to each of those questions. Then consider now from this day and upward. Consider it.

From this day He will bless you. —EBF

Reflect and Respond

Consider your ways. What do you learn? What should you change?

Your favorite scripture in **Haggai**

ZECHARIAH 8:5

**And the streets of the city shall be
full of boys and girls playing.**

When my kids were growing up, they loved to play night games. We would sit out at night and listen to the happy voices and the laughter until those summertime sounds slowly faded away. Those long nights and sweet memories are some of my favorite recollections.

At the time of Zechariah, the rebellion of the children of Israel resulted in their precious city being lost and their futures dimmed. But Zechariah prophesied to a sad, scattered Israel that one day they would enjoy happy lives in Jerusalem again. "I am returned unto Zion, and will dwell in the midst of Jerusalem . . . there shall yet old men and old women dwell in the streets of Jerusalem . . . and the streets of the city shall be full of boys and girls playing in the streets thereof" (Zechariah 8:3–5). Isn't that a perfect description of a happy people?

Reading the Old Testament quickly reveals themes and patterns that might otherwise be missed. How often have we pled with the ancient church to turn to the Lord and enjoy the felicity of blessings He was offering? How often have we been exhausted to read Jehovah's prophets cry repentance again and again on deaf ears? Have you ever said, "Why don't they just repent!?"

The Old Testament ends with a church crumbling in apostasy, but the destruction is accompanied by a promise of a return to the covenants. One day, someone would follow Zechariah's advice: "Turn ye unto me, saith the Lord of hosts, and I will turn unto you. . . . Be ye not as your fathers, unto whom the former prophets have cried, saying . . . Turn ye now from your evil ways, and from your evil doings" (Zechariah 1:3–4). May our own happy summer days always be a reminder of the good life we live as we learn from the past and turn to Him. —EBF

Reflect and Respond

How does repentance lead to happiness?

Your favorite
scripture in
Zechariah

MALACHI 3:10

Open you the windows of heaven . . .

There are several verses in Malachi that we are very familiar with, but hidden within those verses there are two words that I had never noticed until just recently—two words that completely changed my heart on the subject of paying tithes. If you look in the footnotes for verses 8–10 of chapter 3 in Malachi, you will discover the two words I am talking about. The first word is found in the footnote for verse 8, "Will a man rob God?" The word contained in this footnote is *ingratitude.* It leads me to wonder if gratitude has a place in the payment of our tithes. What does gratitude have to do with tithing?

When my husband saw a boy whom we had mentored for half a decade standing on the sidewalk with all of his belongings and realized his family was being evicted and the boy had nowhere to live, he immediately called me to ask, "What should I do with Garett?"

"Bring him home," I said. I'll be honest, I didn't know how long he would make it here, with the boundaries, the structure, the unfamiliar surroundings day in and day out. We took it a day at a time. He started going to church. He was home and in bed by eleven. Slowly, he began turning his life around. He got a job, and he started paying tithing. One day he asked me, "Why do I pay tithing, again? I don't get it. Aren't I supposed to be seeing blessings?" He was serious, thoughtful, trying to understand. "Do you see the blessings?" I asked him. "I don't think so," he replied.

"Do you have a job?" I asked. "Yes." "Have you *ever* had a job before?" "No."

"Do you have a roof over your head? A comfortable place to sleep? Clothes to wear? Do you feel safe here? Welcome? Do you feel happy?" As he begin nodding his head, I asked again, "Do you *see* the blessings?"

He tilted his head, reflecting, and then I watched the understanding come into his eyes.

"I *am* blessed," he said, "I *am* happy. Is that what it feels like when you pay your tithing?" In that moment it became clear to me that gratitude pays a huge part in the payment of our tithes. The Lord asks us to prove Him. He promises to open the windows of heaven, to pour out a blessing that there will not be room enough to receive.

Every so often, in the moments when I remember, after I have filled out the tithing slip and placed it in the little grey envelope, I pause. If I am in a place where it is appropriate, I offer up a silent prayer of gratitude. Ever since I learned the lesson, I have tried to remember to make gratitude an integral part of the payment of tithes.

The second word you will notice in the footnotes is *generosity*. It is linked to the phrase "open you the windows of heaven" (Malachi 3:10). Those verses in Malachi remind us how generous the Lord is with us. It was a story of President Henry D. Moyle, told by President James E. Faust, that taught me that I could be generous with the Lord. "As I grew up out in the Cottonwood area of the Salt Lake Valley, President Henry D. Moyle was our stake president. Years passed and I became bishop of our ward. President Moyle, in the intervening years, was called to the Council of the Twelve and later to the First Presidency. Like the other faithful members of the ward, President Moyle always came to tithing settlement. Invariably each year . . . he always said, 'Bishop, this is a full tithe and a little bit more because that's the way we have been blessed.'"[29]

Just two simple words that become integral to our understanding of paying tithes: *gratitude* and *generosity*. —EBF

Reflect and Respond
What blessings have you experienced from paying your tithes?

Your favorite scripture in Malachi

NOTES

1. Bruce Satterfield, "The Family Under Siege: The Role of Men and Women," Ricks College Education Week presentation, June 7, 2001.
2. Jeffrey R. Holland, "Remember Lot's Wife: Faith Is for the Future," BYU devotional, January 13, 2009.
3. In Truman G. Madsen, *The Highest in Us* (1978), 49.
4. Susan W. Tanner, "My Soul Delighteth in the Things of the Lord," *Ensign*, May 2008.
5. "Praise to the Man," *Hymns of The Church of Jesus Christ of Latter-day Saints* (1985), no. 27.
6. Alfred Edersheim, *Bible History: Old Testament*, 7 vols. (1876–1887), 1:117.
7. Edersheim, *Bible History*, 1:143.
8. Elizabeth Barrett Browning, "Aurora Leigh."
9. Jeffrey R. Holland, "Cast Not Away Therefore Your Confidence," BYU devotional, March 2, 1999.
10. Edersheim, *Bible History*, 2:147–53.
11. Edersheim, *Bible History*, 3:43.
12. Edersheim, *Bible History*, 3:43.
13. Ronald A. Rasband, "Special Experiences," *Ensign*, May 2008.
14. Russell M. Nelson, "Let God Prevail," *Ensign*, November 2020.
15. F. Enzio Busche, "Unleashing the Dormant Spirit," BYU devotional, May 14, 1996.
16. In Edersheim, *Bible History*, 3:121.
17. Edersheim, *Bible History*, 3:138.
18. Don C. Corbett, *Mary Fielding Smith, Daughter of Britain* (1970), v.
19. Joseph B. Wirthlin, "Come What May, and Love It," *Ensign*, November 2008.
20. Boyd K. Packer, "How to Survive in Enemy Territory," *New Era*, April 2012.
21. *Discourses of Brigham Young*, comp. John A. Widtsoe (1954), 243.
22. J. Golden Kimball, in Conference Report, April 1915, 79.
23. Brigham Young, as quoted in James E. Faust, "Standing in Holy Places," *Ensign*, May 2005.
24. Gordon B. Hinckley, "The Good and Faithful Servants," *Ensign*, November 1984; emphasis added.
25. Jeffrey R. Holland, "A Prayer for the Children," *Ensign*, May 2003.
26. James E. Faust, "What I Want My Son to Know before He Leaves on His Mission," *Ensign*, May 1996.
27. Joseph Smith, The Wentworth Letter, available at josephsmithpapers.org/paper-summary/church-history-1-march-1842/4.
28. Henry B. Eyring, "Our Hearts Knit as One," *Ensign*, November 2008.
29. James E. Faust, "Doing the Best Things in the Worst Times," *Ensign*, August 1984.

ABOUT THE AUTHORS

EMILY BELLE FREEMAN is a best-selling author and popular inspirational speaker. She has a deep love of the scriptures, which comes from a desire to find their application in everyday life. She is the author of numerous books, including *Grace Where You Are; Creating a Christ-Centered Home; Closer to Christ;* and *And These Words: An Emily Belle Freeman Scripture Study Journal.* She is a favorite speaker at Time Out for Women and a cohost with David Butler of *Don't Miss This,* a *Come, Follow Me* study channel on YouTube. Her greatest joy comes from spending time with her family. Read more at emilybellefreeman.com and follow Emily on Instagram and Facebook @emilybellefreeman.

DAVID BUTLER'S greatest love is people. His favorite people are his wife, Jenny, and their six darling children. Some of his other loves include good food, spontaneous adventures, Christmas morning, and the sea. David cohosts the popular YouTube scripture study channel *Don't Miss This* with Emily Belle Freeman and is the author of many religious books, including *Ites: An Illustrated Guide to the People in the Book of Mormon; The Peter Potential;* and *Almighty: How the Most Powerful Being in the Universe Is Also Your Loving Father.* Follow him on Instagram @mrdavebutler.

HEALTH CARE POLICY, PERFORMANCE AND FINANCE

Health Care Policy, Performance
and Finance

Strategic Issues in Health Care Management

Edited by

HUW T.O. DAVIES AND MANOUCHE TAVAKOLI

ASHGATE

Published by
Ashgate Publishing Limited
Gower House
Croft Road
Aldershot
Hampshire GU11 3HR
England

Ashgate Publishing Company
Suite 420
101 Cherry Street
Burlington, VT 05401-4405
USA

Ashgate website: http://www.ashgate.com

British Library Cataloguing in Publication Data
International Conference on Strategic Issues in Health Care
Management (5th : 2002 : University of St Andrews)
    Health care policy, performance and finance : strategic
    issues in health care management
    1.Health services administration - Congresses 2.Strategic
    planning - Congresses 3.Medical policy - Congresses
    I.Title II.Davies, Huw T. O. III.Tavakoli, Manouche
    362.1'068

Library of Congress Cataloging-in-Publication Data
International Conference on Strategic Issues in Health Care Management (5th : 2002 :
    University of St. Andrews)
    Health care policy, performance and finance : strategic issues in health care management
    / edited by Huw Davies and Manouche Tavakoli.
        p. cm.
    Proceedings of the 5th International Conference on Strategic issues in Health Care
    Management, held at the University of St. Andrews, Scotland in spring 2002.
    Includes bibliographical references.
    ISBN 0-7546-3865-0
    1. Medical policy--Congresses. 2. Medical care--Quality control--Congresses. 3. Medical
    care--Finance--Congresses. 4. Health services administration--Congresses. I. Davies,
    Huw, 1959- II. Tavakoli, Manouche. III. Title.

RA393.I557 2002
362.1'068--dc22

2003058367

ISBN 0 7546 3865 0

Printed and bound in Great Britain by MPG Books Ltd, Bodmin, Cornwall